Warrior · 26

US Paratrooper 1941–45

Carl Smith · Illustrated by Mike Chappell

First published in Great Britain in 2000 by Osprey Publishing, Elms Court, Chapel Way, Botley, Oxford OX2 9LP, United Kingdom.
Email: info@ospreypublishing.com

CIP Data for this publication is available from the British Library

04 05 06 07 08 10 9 8 7 6 5 4 3

ISBN 1 85532 842 9

Editor: Nikolai Bogdanovic
Design: Paul Kime
Index by Alan Rutter
Originated by Colourpath, London, UK
Printed in China through World Print Ltd

FOR A CATALOGUE OF ALL BOOKS PUBLISHED BY OSPREY MILITARY AND AVIATION PLEASE CONTACT:

The Marketing Manager, Osprey Direct UK,
PO Box 140, Wellingborough, Northants,
NN8 2FA, United Kingdom.
Email: info@ospreydirect.co.uk

The Marketing Manager, Osprey Direct USA,
c/o MBI Publishing, PO Box 1,
729 Prospect Avenue, Osceola, WI 54020, USA.
Email: info@ospreydirectusa.com

www.ospreypublishing.com

Rank abbreviations

Maj Gen = Major General	**Tech Sgt** = Technical Sergeant
Brig Gen = Brigadier General	**Tech 2** = Technician 2nd Grade
Col = Colonel	**S/Sgt** = Staff Sergeant
Lt Col = Lieutenant Colonel	**Tech 3** = Technician 3rd Grade
Maj = Major	**Sgt** = Sergeant
Capt = Captain	**Tech 4** = Technician 4th Grade
1st Lt = 1st Lieutenant	**Corp** = Corporal
2nd Lt = 2nd Lieutenant	**Tech 5** = Technician 5th Grade
M Sgt = Master Sergeant	**Pfc** = Private 1st Class
1st Sgt = 1st Sergeant	**Pvt** = Private
Tech 1 = Technician 1st Grade	

Editor's note

Special thanks go to Gordon Rottman for his technical advice and expertise, and his contribution to the color plates and commentaries.

Artist's note

Readers may care to note that the original paintings from which the color plates in this book were prepared are available for private sale. All reproduction copyright whatsoever is retained by the Publishers. All enquiries should be addressed to:

Mike Chappell, 27 Nelson Street, Deal, Kent CT14 6DR, UK

The Publishers regret that they can enter into no correspondence upon this matter.

Glossary

Absent Without Leave (AWOL) = a soldier who has left base without permission or a pass. A lesser status than desertion.

Blowout = A ripped parachute panel that allows air to spill out of the chute too quickly, and which subsequently affects the paratrooper's ability to control it.

Cigarette Roll = When a reserve parachute is opened and wraps around an uninflated main parachute (see Streamer).

Drop Zone (DZ) = An area where paratroopers are supposed to land.

GIR = Glider Infantry Regiment.

Jump School = Popular name for the Airborne Training Center at Fort Benning.

Jump Wings = The pewter wings, with a parachute superimposed, that were presented to members of the 501st on 15 March 1941 and have been in use ever since. Bailey, Banks & Biddle Company of Philadelphia produced the wings from a design by Capt William P. Yarborough.

Landing Zone (LZ) = An area where gliders or aircraft are supposed to land in order to debark troops or materiel, or rendezvous with ground personnel.

Panel = One of 28 pie-shaped sections (wider at the bottom than the top) that constituted a parachute. The panels did not meet at the top, where a circular 18-inch (45 cm) aperture formed the apex of the parachute. Shroud lines connected each panel corner to a riser.

PFAB = Parachute Field Artillery Battalion.

PIB = Parachute Infantry Battalion.

PIR = Parachute Infantry Regiment.

Risers = The four web straps, two to either side of the harness, one front and one back. Each riser has seven shroud lines attached to it and also connects to the harness. In order to control the rate and direction of descent, a paratrooper grasps and tugs risers, spilling air from specific areas of the parachute and thus affecting his descent.

Shroud (suspension) lines = The individual, bound groups of silken or nylon twine with a covering sheath that control the parachute canopy. Shroud lines connect the canopy to the risers. On a standard American World War II parachute, there were 28 shroud lines.

Straight Legs = Derogatory term used by paratroopers (who were allowed to wear bloused jump boots with Class A uniforms) to describe all non-airborne branches of the service.

Streamer = A deployed parachute that has failed to inflate or a paratrooper whose chute has failed to open.

US PARATROOPER 1941–45

In this commercial photograph, which many paratroopers bought and sent to loved ones, the jumper pulls on his left front riser prior to landing. (Author's collection)

INTRODUCTION: DEATH FROM ABOVE

General Kurt Student's German paratroopers (*Fallschirmjagers*, to give them their German name) and their glider offensive on Eban Emael in May 1940 made the world aware of a new threat: death from above. Attacking units could now be delivered to objectives with astounding speed, and armies no longer needed to telegraph their moves in advance. The potential for airborne troops was soon recognized.

Ironically, it was the Germans' costly assault on the Greek island of Crete on 20 May 1940 that caused the United States to look at increasing their airborne forces. Over 10,500 German paratroopers and glider infantry hit Crete, spearheading an invasion that was to be supported by seaborne troops. However, the German seaborne units were turned back by British sea power and never reached Crete. It was left to the airborne forces to carry the entire assault.

The Germans paid a heavy price, but Crete was theirs. The British withdrew 17,000 survivors on 30 May 1940 and left others trapped behind. General Student proclaimed German losses (estimated to be between 30 and 44 per cent) to be excessive, and he called Crete the 'grave' of the German paratroop corps. By contrast, America's Gen George C. Marshall believed that there had been no other way to assault the seemingly impregnable island of Crete. The seed of the American Airborne Division had been sewn.

AIRBORNE CHRONOLOGY

29 April 1928 – At Kelly Field, Texas, a machine-gun team parachutes, successfully lands, and makes its landed gun operational.

1931 – An artillery battery is airlifted across the Isthmus of Panama in the Canal Zone.

1932 – An infantry unit lands behind 'enemy' forces during a maneuver at Fort DuPont, Delaware.

May 1939 – The Chief of Infantry proposes the formation of a detachment of air infantry. The Army Air Corps desires that paratroopers be placed under its control as 'air grenadiers'.

1 September 1939 – Germany invades Poland.

Late 1939 – The fledgling parachute unit is put under control of the infantry (AGF).

2 January 1940 – The War Department has the Chief of Infantry conduct a feasibility study of paratroopers and the air transport of infantry and materials.

April 1940 – A plan to form a test platoon of paratroopers is approved.

9 April 1940 – German paratroops and glider infantry capture Eban Emael at the beginning of the Blitzkrieg. German airborne troops land at Oslo Airport.

25 June 1940 – The commandant of the Infantry School at Fort Benning is ordered to organize a parachute test platoon, calling upon volunteers from the 29th Infantry Regiment.

1 July 1940 – The first parachute test platoon of 48 men is formed at Fort Benning. Two hundred men had volunteered from the 29th Infantry Regiment.

16 August 1940 – At Lawson Field, Georgia, the first official drop of US paratroopers takes place.

29 August 1940 – The first mass jump of US paratroopers.

September 1940 – The Second Division is directed to study the landing of US airborne troops. Exercises are conducted on Lawson Field at Fort Benning.

1 October 1940 – The 501st Parachute Infantry Battalion is formed from the cader of the Test Platoon.

1 July 1941 – A second parachute battalion, the 502nd, is formed.

1 August 1941 – Lieutenant-Colonel Gavin arrives at Fort Benning to begin paratroop training.

7 December 1941 – Japan bombs Pearl Harbor.

8 December 1941 – The US declares war on Japan.

11 December 1941 – Germany and Italy declare war on the United States.

24 February 1942 – 1st Battalion is redesignated as the 501st PIB.

25 March 1942 – 82nd Airborne Division is formed.

15 August 1942 – 101st Airborne Division is formed.

2 November 1942 – The 501st is deactivated in Australia and its components are redesignated as the 2nd Battalion 503rd Parachute Infantry Regiment.

7–8 November 1942 – Overnight US paratroopers of the 503rd PIR under Raff leave England and fly to Oran where only 18 per cent actually jump and assault their objective. By the end of the day, the airfield at Oran is under Allied control.

8 November 1942 – Operation Torch (Allied landings in French North Africa) begins.

15 November 1942 – Raff's 503rd assault an airfield near Tebbessa, Tunisia. A new 1st Battalion 501st is activated at Camp Tocoa, Georgia.

25 February 1943 – 11th Airborne Division is formed.

15 April 1943 – 17th Airborne Division is formed.

20 April 1943 – 82nd moves to Massachusetts en route to Africa.

10 May 1943 – 82nd arrives at Casablanca.

9–10 July 1943 – Operation Husky: Paratroopers jump near Syracuse in the campaign for Sicily. This staggered four-day jump was the worst airborne disaster of the war. Sixty-nine Wacos and three Horsas go down at sea because of extraordinarily high winds, at a cost of 605 lives from the British 1st Air Landing Brigade (which numbered 1,690 men) in the first

This calling card contained the lyrics to the song of the 82nd Airborne Division, 'The All-American Soldier'. The card was given out to members of the unit. (Author's collection)

"The All-American" Soldier

Words by Sgt. Carl Sigman

(Chorus)

We're All American, and proud to be;
For we're the soldiers of liberty.
Some ride the gliders through the enemy,
Others are sky paratroopers.
We're All American, and fight we will
Till all the guns of the foe are still
Airborne, from skies of blue
We're coming through——
Make Your Jumps, Take Your Bumps
Let's Go!

Interlude

Put on your boots,
Your parachutes——
Get all those gliders ready
To attack today;
For we'll be gone
Into the dawn
To fight 'em all
The 82nd way - - - Yes

(Repeat Chorus)

day. Members of the 82nd's 505th PIR (3,405 men), who were to support Patton's 7th Army near Gela, are dropped as much as 50 miles (80 km) off course in 25–30 mile per hour (40–48 km/h) winds. Allied ships open fire and eight C47s are destroyed by naval antiaircraft fire, at a cost of 140 airborne lives.

11 July 1943 – Operation Husky: Despite Gen Clark's orders to hold fire, when the 504th PIR jump, shore batteries open fire and naval batteries join in, destroying 23 C47s and damaging 37 more, killing 334 paratroopers and glidermen. Some are shot by 'friendly fire' as they descend, while others land near German armored units and are slaughtered. At Biazza Ridge, Col Gavin and a hastily assembled unit of 505th PIR and 307th Airborne Engineer Battalion halt the advance of the Herman Goering Division.

20 July 1943 – The 1st Special Service Force, later to be nicknamed the Devil's Brigade by the Germans, is formed under Brig Gen Frederick. The unit is a mixture of 2,300 US and Canadian paratroops, mountain-troops, and winter-war specialists.

22 July 1943 – Americans enter Palermo. A week later they are supported by the British 78th Division attacking toward the city.

Supply sergeants helped to keep the army rolling along. This picture taken in Germany shows Lts Haven, Guillart and Smith of the 508th in fur-collared AAF bomber jackets. A supply sergeant who had managed to trade with another unit had procured these jackets, which were not Airborne issue. (Author's collection)

13 August 1943 – The 13th Airborne Division is formed.

14 August 1943 – Sicily falls to the Allied armies at a cost of 45 transports, 73 gliders, and 1,100 men killed in the air. Consequently the US Navy drops its plans for air-delivery of Marines.

17 August 1943 – Patton enters Messina hours before the British. The battle for Sicily ends.

5 September 1943 – The 503rd PIR jumps at Nazdeb on the Markham River, New Guinea, landing in grass ten to 12 feet (3–3.6 m) tall. The 503rd cut off Japanese troops who were attempting to withdraw from Lae and Salamauam and capture a vital airstrip. Australian units from Tsili Tsili join the 503rd, and the entire Australian 7th Division is to be flown in. The success of this attack allayed US fears of excessive loss of life in airborne operations, as seen in Sicily.

9 September 1943 – In the Salerno Campaign, the Allied amphibious invasion stalls on the beach; the British 1st Airborne Division lands at Taranto and two days later takes Brindisi.

13 September 1943 – In an airlift, the 504th PIR and 325th GIR land near Paestum and defeat three German panzer divisions, much of the combat is hand-to-hand.

14 September 1943 – The 504th drops 1,900 paratroopers and the 325th GIR land by sea to take part in the struggle. Most of the 509th PIB jumps at Avellino, but the troops are scattered and do not complete their mission – of 641 only 531 make it back to Allied lines. Part of the 509th PIB participates in the seaborne attack on a

German radar installation at Ventotene, 18 miles (29 km) off shore. The mission is a success.

November 1943 – The Devil's Brigade takes part in the Aleutians Campaign

2 December 1943 – The Devil's Brigade breaches the Winter Line; Brig Gen Frederick loses 532 men in an assault on an 'unassailable' position that infantry had failed to take. The 1st Special Service Force is later transferred to Anzio.

22 January 1944 – At Anzio, Allied landings begin, and the 509 PIB and 504 Regimental Combat Team (RCT) – which comprised the 504th PIR plus 376th PFAR, and Co.C of the 307th Airborne Engineer Battalion – spearhead the amphibious invasion of Anzio.

10 April 1944 – the 504th RCT is withdrawn from Anzio and sent to England to train for D-Day.

4 June 1944 – The Devil's Brigade and other units of the 88th Division enter Rome.

6 June 1944 – Operation Overlord: American actions on D-Day see a combined force of 18,000 men of the 82nd and 101st Airborne, plus the British 6th Airborne Division, drop behind German lines to disrupt communications and stop German reserves from reaching the beaches. American losses were 2,500 on D-Day, and 7,400 by the time US paratroops were removed from France and returned to England for training prior to Operation Market Garden.

3 July 1944 – 1st Battalion of the 503rd PIR jumps at Noemfoor Island to take Kamiriz Airfield in the New Guinea Campaign. Despite heavy casualties they take their objective. The 2nd Battalion joins them the following day.

15 August 1944 – Operation Dragoon: Allied troops land to assault Cannes and Toulon. Brig Gen Frederick's 1st Airborne Task Force (ATF) includes the 509th PIB, 517th PIR, 596th Airborne Engineers Co., 460th PFAB, 551st PIB, 463rd PFAB, 887th Airborne Engineers Co., 512 Airborne Signal Co., 550th PIB, AT Co., 442nd Infantry Regiment (composed of Nisei, Japanese Americans), and the British 2nd Independent Parachute Brigade. The Task Force moves on the objectives of Le Muy and Le Mitan with air corps and glider landings. Most of the casualties were among the glider troops. By the end of the operation more than 90 per cent of the glider force is unsalvageable.

25 August 1944 – Paris is liberated.

28 August 1944 – Marseilles and Toulon fall to the ATF. Although one third of the airborne forces were lost, the objective (the French Mediter-ranean) was taken in 40 per cent of the time allocated. Airborne missions were declared a success.

9 September 1944 – The Allies control the French Mediterranean.

17 September 1944 – Operation Market Garden: In a daylight assault, three bridges (at Eindhoven,

At war's end, a paratrooper demonstrates the proper way to stand in the doorway prior to jumping. The C-47 is already in silver (post-war) livery, and the men wear the post-1943 issue army fatigues.
(Author's collection)

Nijmegen, and Arnhem) become airborne targets. The objectives are to be taken by the American 101st, American 82nd, and British 1st Airborne Divisions, respectively. The American objectives are taken, but the Arnhem bridge is not, as the British armor fails to break through and link up with the British 1st Airborne Division. At Eindhoven, the 101st rebuilds a bridge within 12 hours of the Germans destroying it. At Nijmegen, members of the 82nd suffer 50 per cent losses as they cross the river by boat to take their objective.

21 September 1944 – Although the British XXX Corps attacks from Nijmegen, British airborne troops are forced out of Arnhem. The Polish Parachute Brigade is dropped two miles (3.25 km) south of the British paratroops – but they are too late.

24 September 1944 – The XXX Corps reaches the south bank of the Rhine west of Arnhem, they cross the Rhine to the southwest at Nijmegen.

25 September 1944 – The decision is made to evacuate the British paratroopers in Arnhem, taking them across the Rhine in small boats. Of the 10,000 who landed, only 2,400 escape. Nearly 1,100 are killed and a further 6,400 are taken prisoner.

16 December 1944 – The Battle of the Bulge begins in the Ardennes.

17 December 1944 – The Allies plug holes in their line using the 82nd, 101st, 509th, 517th, 550th, and 551st Airborne units, which are brought to the front overland.

19 December 1944 – US airborne forces hold the crossroads at Bastogne and St. Vith.

22 December 1944 – St. Vith falls to the Germans. General McAuliff replies: 'Nuts!' after Gen Heinrich von Luettwitz, his German counterpart, asks him to surrender.

26 December 1944 – The US 4th Armored Division reaches the Americans and shortly thereafter, Patton's Third Army arrives to turn the tide. During the Bulge, 61 Wacos come under extreme enemy fire, but still manage to land badly needed medics and supplies at Bastogne. The first Waco to land was from the 96th Squadron of the 440th Troop Carrier Group. The final 15 gliders are shot down on approach. Airdrops completed the re-supply of the airborne and other isolated American units. Without the airborne and gliders, Bastogne may have been lost. The price the airborne paid was high: nearly 20,000 lost their lives. Of the 509th PIR, only two officers and 47 enlisted men were still fit for duty after the battle.

16 January 1945 – The Battle of the Bulge ends as the 1st and 3rd Allied Armies link at Houffalize.

31 January 1945 – Two regiments of Gen Swing's 11th Airborne Division (without the 511th PIR) land by sea near Manila.

This paratrooper, who is photographed outside a barracks at Fort Benning, wears a 1942-issue jump suit. His uniform and equipment, plus a belt of .50-caliber ammunition, suggest he is a member of a machine-gun crew. He could be a Nisei (which would date the photograph to 1943 to 1944). Nisei were volunteers from the Japanese-American community who enlisted following a request from Franklin D. Roosevelt in 1943. These men, who served in Italy and other European theaters, made up the greater part of the 442nd Infantry. (Airborne & Special Operations Museum, Ft. Bragg, NC)

3 February 1945 – In a three-wave attack, Swing's 511th PIR assaults Tagaytay Ridge while other American troops advance from seaward, beginning a month-long series of hand-to-hand and house-to-house fights.

9 February 1945 – The 11th Airborne attacks Japanese units southeast of Manila near Nielsen Field.

13 February 1945 – The 11th Airborne takes Nichols Field near Cavite.

16 February 1945 – The 503rd RCT drops on the 'fortress-island' of Corregidor in Manila Bay with multiple passes from its aircraft. Only six men from a stick could drop at any one time during a simultaneous sea assault. Fighting is intense in the tunnels and gun emplacements of the island.

23 February 1945 – Company B of the 511th PIR, 11th Airborne Division, jumps 30 miles (48 km) behind Japanese lines to take the Los Banos prison camp, freeing 2,147 Allied prisoners of war held there. This is regarded by many as the most successful airborne mission of World War II.

26 February 1945 – Corregidor falls to American troops. The cost: 1,200 casualties, 445 of them fatalities. Only 19 of the 5,000 or so Japanese troops who held the island were captured alive.

2 March 1945 – Gen MacArthur returns ('I shall return...') to the Philippines.

3 March 1945 – Manila falls to US troops.

9 March 1945 – US 9th Armored Division takes the Bridge at Remagen, enabling Allied forces to cross the Rhine.

22 March 1945 – Patton's Third Army crosses the Rhine at Oppenheim.

23 March 1945 – Operation Varsity: More than 1,600 C47s and 1,300 Waco, Horsa, and Hamilcar gliders, fly across the Rhine and drop the 20,000 men of the US 17th and British 6th Airborne Divisions on Wesel. The US 13th Airborne Division does not jump as there are not enough aircraft available to transport them. The cost of the operation in airborne lives is almost 2,500 paratroopers and glidermen killed. (More than lost by the 82nd and 101st on D-Day.)

29 March 1945 – Negros Island, Philippines, the 503rd PIR and other US troops assault by sea. Nine weeks later the island falls to American troops.

13 April 1945 – American forces land on Fort Drum ('the concrete battleship') in Manila Bay, which is held by Japanese troops. The Japanese button up and the Americans pour gasoline down air vents and light it. The fire burns for five days.

26 April 1945 – The American Division lands at Negros to help pacify the island.

7 May 1945 – The war in Europe ends. The 82nd Airborne is designated as part of the Allied Occupation Army.

10 June 1945 – The 508th (of the 82nd) takes up its post-war duty station at Frankfurt-am-Main, Germany where Gen Dwight D. Eisenhower sets up SHAEF Headquarters. The 508th was to provide security at SHAEF.

23 June 1945 – Paratroop landing of the 1st Battalion, 511th PIR, 11th Airborne Division near Aparri at the mouth of the Cagayan River on Luzon's north coast.

July 1945 – The 82nd Airborne enters Berlin.

10 August 1945 – Japan agrees to cease hostilities after the bombings of Hiroshima and Nagasaki.

15 August 1945 – Japan agrees to surrender.

2 September 1945 – The Japanese sign the surrender aboard the USS *Missouri*; the 11th Airborne Division enters Japan where it will remain the main occupation force.

16 September 1945 – 17th Airborne Division deactivated at Camp Myles Standish, Massachusetts.

25 February 1946 – The 13th Airborne Division deactivated at Fort Bragg, North Carolina.

RECRUITMENT AND TRAINING

This photograph shows Pvts John M. Welch and Elmer T. Bryant of the 508th standing in front of their squad tent on base. Pvt Bryant was KIA in the Normandy invasion and Pvt Bryant was listed as MIA on 9 July 1944, but does not appear in the unit history as having been killed in action, and so presumably survived. (Author's collection)

Nobody accidentally ended up in the Airborne during World War II. To become a paratrooper, a man either had to be actively recruited, or currently a member of the US military. Even then, he still had to request Jump School training. Paratroopers were the elite of the US Army in World War II, and they knew it. They were the only servicemen who were allowed to wear their highly polished jump boots with class-A uniforms. As a result, they became known as 'baggy-pants', and they looked down upon their less fortunate 'straight-leg' cousins, who were not permitted to wear their class-A slacks bloused into their boots.

At the start of World War II, there were two routes a man could follow to join the military. He could either volunteer, or take his chances with the draft. The draft (or conscription as it was officially known) was the process by which any citizen over 18 years old could be called-up for military duty. A man who volunteered for service joined at the time of his choosing. Conscripts, however, were called-up at the behest of the draft board, and although they could request a specific branch of service, requests were only honored if positions were open, otherwise men were allocated where the military's need was greatest. A man was generally eligible for the draft until his 25th birthday. If his number was pulled, he received a 'compliments of Uncle Sam' letter that told him when and where to report.

At the recruiting station, a volunteer was shown the various branches of military service and had a chance to volunteer for units that needed men. In late 1942, new recruiters, who wore spit-shined, hard-toed Corcoran jump boots, began appearing at recruiting stations. They were there to find suitable recruits for the Airborne. The recruiters, with their elite uniforms, special training, and *esprit de corps*, appealed to many young men. Those who were interested were asked to perform a series of backward and forward rolls and were graded as suitable or unsuitable depending on their performance. Some recruiters even approached members of national guard units. The Airborne, like the Marines, wanted 'a few good men'. Quality, not quantity, was their unwritten credo.

BASIC TRAINING

There were two kinds of basic training: traditional and the newer, cadre style. In traditional training, a recruit was sent to basic for 13 weeks, then went to his unit either directly or via an advanced school. Prior to the development of the Airborne, most soldiers went through traditional training.

Paratroopers, like all soldiers, had their gear frequently inspected to make sure that it was serviceable and clean. Here, the gear is displayed on a bunk that has had its head and footboards folded underneath the frame and springs. This gave the unit a length of around six feet (1.82 m) and a height of six inches (15.2 cm). (Author's collection)

The Airborne was particularly strong in the use of cadre, utilizing a nucleus of men from an existing unit to create a new unit. The cadre would also be used to train the new unit's recruits in basic military skills (basic training), although the cadre would itself first be sent to Jump School for four weeks of airborne training. When trainees of the new unit subsequently went through Jump School at Fort Benning, those who were physically or psychologically unfit were weeded out. The cadre would become officers and NCOs of the new unit upon its completion of Jump School.

The cadre of a new unit would be treated like any other recruits, regardless of rank, while at Jump School. To graduate, they had to successfully complete five jumps and, to remain qualified as paratroopers, they would need to make at least one jump every three months. Cadre received intensive instruction on how to train recruits.

The 508th Parachute Infantry Regiment is a typical example of a cadre unit. The cadre went to Jump School at Fort Benning, but moved their recruits to Camp Blanding, Florida, for basic training. For 13 weeks, the 508th's recruits learned soldiering skills in a basic training course set up by their cadre. Upon graduating from basic training, both the cadre and trainees moved back to Fort Benning for Jump School. As most officers and cadre had already received jump training, they were given additional training (such as detailed demolitions or other courses). The unit's recruits, meanwhile, were turned over to drill instructors and drill sergeants for four weeks of intensive paratroop training. After graduation from Jump School, the unit was reunited and moved to Camp Mackall, North Carolina or Fort Bragg, also in North Carolina, for additional training and maneuvers, which would help hone the paratroopers' recently acquired skills.

QUARTERS AND GEAR

Recruits were first gathered at local induction stations, from where they were sent to major induction centers via train or bus. After working their way through a mountain of paperwork, new recruits were assigned to basic training companies. These companies were composed of platoons, which were further broken down into squads. After 13 weeks of basic training and four weeks of Jump School, paratroopers were sent to their companies to work within their teams and practice individual skills.

There were numerous basic training camps around the United States, and some, such as Fort Benning, still exist today. Upon arrival at training camp, the new recruit received his first military haircut, whether he needed it or not:

'Want those sideburns?' the barber would ask.

'Yep,' the inductee replied.

'Then hold out your hand,' the barber would quip, as he cut the inductee's hair down to a fine stubble with sweeping motions of his clippers.

Next, recruits were assigned barracks, and then they were marched (one of the few times they marched rather than ran) to the supply room to get boots, clothing, fatigues, and other issued gear. Each recruit signed documents verifying that he had been given a basic issue. Everything was signed for and accounted for in the army. Recruits soon learned that there was much truth behind the army cliché: 'If it moves, salute it; if it doesn't move, sign for it. If it disappears, pay for it'.

New uniforms were dumped into the recruit's waiting arms, then stuffed into duffel bags. Recruits were marched back to their barracks to straighten out their foot and wall lockers, put away their clothing, and clean their living quarters.

Many of the barracks used during World War II are still standing, and some are still in use today. They were arranged near to a training company headquarters and positioned with their front doors facing a central walkway. Most barracks were two stories high, painted a yellowish tan color, and had a green or black tarpaper roof. A barracks' rectangular building would sport a single door at either of its narrow ends. Over the door was a balcony with a wooden ladder, which was fastened to the building as an emergency fire escape. On the right side of the building's front was a boiler room with two furnaces – a small one for hot water and a larger one for heating during winter. Near the training battalion barracks complex was a day room for soldiers' use, a mess hall, and a company headquarters, which was attached to the supply room.

To one side of the barracks' front door was a shower room with lavatory. Sinks underneath mirrors lined the interior wall of this room, while showers lined the outside wall. Toilets and urinals, without stalls for privacy, took up the rest of the room. Opposite the shower room was a flight of stairs that led up to the second floor. Beneath the stairs was a single room for a NCO. The rest of the downstairs interior was a large area called a squad bay. This area was broken-up only by uprights that supported the rafters. Bunks, footlockers, and wall lockers lined the central aisle of the squad bay. Upstairs were two rooms at the head of the stairs followed by a similar squad bay. The barracks' floor was usually brown linoleum – a surface that could be highly shined. The walls were often the same yellowish tan as the outside of the building and they were rarely insulated.

Down the central aisle were several one-gallon fruit cans (empties – with labels removed – that had been collected from the mess hall). These cans were filled with sand and used for smokers to put their cigarette butts in. They could also be used as emergency fire extinguishers on a small fire. Each morning cigarette butts were dumped from cans prior to inspection.

Recruits were assigned bunks, either a lower or an upper. Bunks were arranged 'head to toe', meaning that if the bunkmate above or next to you had his head to the wall, your head was to the central aisle of the barracks. When double-bunks were used, 'downstairs' bunkmates, to both your left and right, would have their heads to the wall, whereas upstairs mates would have their heads to the aisle. This head to toe arrangement, with both upper and lower alternating, was employed to prevent the spread of infectious diseases.

Every recruit had two blankets. Beds were made with two sheets, and the bottom sheet was tucked in with four hospital corners. The top sheet

Pathfinders in plane number 18 (5 June 1944). Seated: air crew – all unknown. Kneeling (left to right): unknown; unknown; unknown; unknown; Pfc Arnold H. Martin (KIA, Bronze Star); Pfc Fayette O. Richardson (Bronze Star); unknown; Pvt Ralph W. Nicholson (KIA, Bronze Star); unknown. Standing: 2nd Lt Edward J. Czepinski (KIA, Bronze Star); Pfc Warren C. Jeffers (Bronze Star); Tech Sgt 5 Francis M. Lamoureaux (Bronze Star); Pfc Charles H. Rogers (Bronze Star); unknown; Pvt E. Stott (HQ3); Cpl Charles F. Calvert (Bronze Star); unknown; Sgt Robert V. Barbiaux (Bronze Star); 2nd Lt Gene H. Williams (KIA, Bronze Star). (508th PIR Museum, Camp Blanding, FL)

had hospital corners at the foot of the bed. The blanket was put on the bed with the initials 'US' positioned in the center and right-reading from the foot of the bed. The blanket also had hospital corners at the foot, was pulled tight, tucked into the sides, and then the top sheet was turned down over it for six to eight inches (18 to 20 cm) and tucked tightly underneath. The second blanket was folded in half with the initials 'US' visible and right reading from the bottom. The pillow was placed on the bed and then a special blanket – called a dust cover – was put over it. The dust cover had hospital corners at the top, and was tucked tight. When the bed was made correctly, a sergeant was able to bounce a quarter on it to show that it was tight.

Many recruits had their beds torn up before their eyes and were berated for having a cover that the sergeant couldn't bounce a quarter on. Recruits soon learned to sit on the closed cover of their footlocker, rather than their bunkmate's bed. Hard words or even harder fists would quickly remind the forgetful.

Each recruit had a footlocker, which was positioned either at the end of the bed (in the case of downstairs bunkmates) or beneath the lower bunk (in the case of upstairs bunkmates). Footlockers were made of ¼-inch (6-mm) plywood, measured 32 in (80 cm) wide by 16 in (40 cm) deep and stood nearly 12 in (30 cm) high. They were reinforced with metal external 'L' brackets at the sides and had common leaf hinges, which were riveted to the back and top. A central metal hasp, positioned at the top edge of the locker's front fastened footlockers. This hasp was fitted over a 'U' eyelet on the outside front wall, through which a padlock could be placed. The top shelf was divided down the middle, forming two 16-inch (40-cm) wide side-by-side open compartments. Other equipment was stored in wall lockers at the head or side of the bed. These lockers were metal, with ventilated doors, and were in a style similar to those found at schools and train-stations.

During inspections, clothing, issue gear, and personal hygiene items were displayed on the bunk. There is a correct way to display gear in a footlocker, using a towel (to cover the bottom of the shelf) beneath the razor, blades, shaving soap and mug, toothpaste and toothbrush. Similarly, t-shirts, underwear, extra fatigues, extra belts, and handkerchiefs were to be displayed in a peculiarly military fashion. Many recruits heard their sergeant bellow: 'There are three ways of doing things, the right way, the wrong way, and the military way.'

Extra boots and shoes were displayed under the bunk, with those belonging to the bottom bunk's occupant facing the side of the bed and closest to the center aisle. The occupant of the upper bunk was to position his boots to the head of the bed. Field jackets and dress uniforms were hung with their fronts facing left in wall lockers. All footgear, fatigue blouses and trousers were generally marked with the owner's service number, whereas underclothing and socks (which were regarded as interchangeable) were not.

Field gear was issued later. However, before recruits got helmets, shelter halves, and tent pegs, they had to learn to march and salute. The issue duffel bag was stenciled with the recruit's last name, first name, middle initial, and service number. Recruits were given service numbers when inducted and told to memorize them. 'Forget your name,' many a NCO intoned, 'but remember your number.' For many years, service

The Airborne officers in this photograph wear class-A uniforms with bloused jump boots. The man on the right wears a short issue officer's overcoat (second pattern, wool, no belt) similar in style and weight to the famous Navy Peacoat. (Airborne & Special Operations Museum, Ft. Bragg, NC)

numbers had prefixes (such as RA for regular army, US for conscripts, AR for Army Reserve, NG for National Guard and O for officer), but this practice changed during the Vietnam War, when all personnel used social security numbers in lieu of service numbers.

BASIC TRAINING: THE REALITY

The purpose of basic training was to rid a man of his civilian habits, replacing them with the military way of doing things. Basic training was also intended to make the recruit physically fit. The first day of training would frequently see a drill sergeant, dressed in immaculate fatigues and World War I campaign hat, line up his charges and eye them as if they were distasteful criminals. His boots would be highly shined, reflecting the sunlight, as did his spun-shined hat brass and belt buckle. By action as well as word, drill sergeants set an example.

Phrases such as, 'You call that clean?' and, 'You call those boots shined?' would frequently screech from the mouths of drill sergeants in the direction of new recruits. There was no correct answer, and in addition to cleaning the area or polishing his boots, the offending inductee was frequently rewarded with additional push-ups. 'Drop and give me 20,' the drill instructor might growl at the hapless recruit. The inductee would also discover the truth of the adage, 'Hurry up and wait'. Inductees ran, quick marched, or double-timed everywhere. It was wartime, and everyone seemed to be in a hurry. Once the recruits reached their destination, they stood in military lines until the instructor arrived and told them to be seated in bleachers or on the ground. If the drill sergeant was in a good mood, he let the men stand 'at ease' instead of ramrod straight. Later in training, when the men were more 'military', the drill sergeant might let them fall out (in place) to: 'Smoke 'em if you got 'em'.

During basic training a recruit underwent weeks of intensive physical and mental training. He was also introduced to the basic military skills, i.e., proper military dress, military etiquette, military life, and working as a member of a team. Every member of the US Army is a rifleman, meaning he is trained and proficient with a rifle. He is classified and earns a medal as Expert, Sharpshooter, or Marksman, depending on how well he scores on the firing range. After firing, trainees are taught to give their weapons a rudimentary clean.

Drill sergeants accompanied their men to all classes. Many classes were held in outdoor classrooms with raised stages. The drill sergeants would march or jog their men to the class and, although another drill sergeant would usually take over instruction, he would roam around his men, correcting their performance. In learning situations, the drill sergeant helped soldiers grasp the basics of dissembling the Garand rifle, or the correct way to shoulder, port, or trail arms. Close order drill was heavily emphasized during the first weeks of training, as was physical exercise. If nothing else, the inductees would look like soldiers by the end of their training.

The daily routine

Company mess halls served three meals a day. Soldiers could usually have milk and/or coffee with every meal. Sunday supper was usually sandwiches of cold cuts but lunch tended to be a hot meal. Many recruits slept in and missed breakfast on Sunday. Most meals were served hot and eaten off metal trays. Soldiers were expected to eat what they were given. A staple was chipped beef on toast, and it was served with such frequency that it was dubbed SOS (Same Old XXXX or Stuff on a Shingle). When a soldier finished his meal, he scraped the scraps off his tray and into a waiting metal garbage can, turned his tray and silverware in to be washed, and had a few minutes to light up a cigarette, write a letter, or straighten his area and gear.

A typical day would see a soldier rise with the sun, exercise, eat breakfast, follow company duty until 0800 hours, and then attend classes until 1200 hours. After morning training, he had an hour for lunch. At 1300 hours, training began again and lasted until 1700 hours when the recruit returned to his company area for supper. Until lights out at 2100 hours, the soldier could take care of personal needs, shower, write letters, do company duty, or relax.

This photograph taken in 1943 shows a member of the 542nd Parachute Infantry Battalion (PIB) posing beside the unit's Headquarters sign. The area around the base was carefully policed. (Airborne & Special Operations Museum, Ft. Bragg, NC)

Usually soldiers followed the same routine Monday through Friday. On Saturdays, recruits worked until 1300 hours. On Sunday, men without passes were confined to the barracks or company area – unless they attended chapel services. Church services were between 0800 and 1200 hours, and generally soldiers attended because those remaining in the barracks were often pulled for company details. Recruits learned that if you made yourself scarce on your 'free' time, you could generally avoid getting pulled for ad hoc police details, fire detail, or for use as a company runner.

OFF DUTY

Most trainees found it difficult to adjust to a life in which they were not permitted to move around freely. Someone had to know where they were at all times. That way, if their unit was called up, they could be located quickly. When leaving the company area, soldiers had to sign out in the company day book (which was kept in company headquarters), giving their destination and length of stay (in hours). Soldiers were accountable for every minute of their day. If a man wanted to leave the base and go to town when he had no duties, he had to get a pass from the company headquarters. Rarely more than half or two-thirds of a unit got a pass (for short, one to two day absences) and few men were granted leave (usually an absence from the unit in excess of three days).

If a soldier was stopped by military police outside the base and did not have a pass on him (whether he had been granted one or not), he was charged with being Absent Without Leave (AWOL). Small infractions were regarded as a company offense and were punished with extra company duty, a fine, a demotion to the next pay grade, or partial

The officers and NCOs of the 508th read their weekly *Red Devil* newspaper before going on guard duty. This picture is taken at the 508th's offices at Frankfurt-am-Main. (Author's collection)

forfeiture of pay. For lengthier absences, a soldier could be sent to the guardhouse.

Paratroopers trained hard but they also played hard. General Gavin's men were clones of him. Bill Moorman commented on the differences between Ridgeway, Taylor, and Gavin saying: 'Ridgeway would cut your throat and then burst into tears. Taylor would cut your throat and think nothing about it. Gavin would cut your throat and then laugh.'

Phoenix City, Alabama, was the destination for many paratroopers with passes. Long-time proximity to the military base saw to it that Phoenix City developed a somewhat worldly atmosphere. There a paratrooper could find a hot meal, a drink, gambling, and female companionship. Prostitution flourished in Phoenix, as it did near most military bases. There were also the inevitable drunken brawls, which were punished by partial forfeiture of pay, extra duty, or a short stint in the guardhouse for more severe infractions.

Fights were rarely one-on-one, as the honor of the unit was at stake. Often the CO of an outfit would be called upon to come down to a bar or roadhouse to bail out his men. Soldiers were punished, but they took it with pride, because they had pride in their unit. If they got into fights, paratroopers reasoned, it was because others were jealous of their status. Many paratroopers sewed a silver dollar under the parachute patch on their garrison cap, this was said to be emergency funds, but its real purpose was to make an impression on an antagonist when it was slapped in his face.

When one paratrooper was arrested for having sex with a woman on the grounds of the courthouse in Phoenix City, the base CO asked Gen Gavin what he was going to do with the man. He replied that, instead of punishing him, they should give the paratrooper a medal, as they were asking him to give his life for his country. The soldier received only light punishment.

It wasn't merely enlisted men who got drunk and rowdy, officers did, too. On more than one occasion MPs were called to the officers' club because paratrooper officers were trying to top one another by jumping from progressively greater heights, starting from the bandstand, then the balcony, and finally from a second story bathroom window.

Missing a formation or a roll call by one minute, technically, made a man AWOL. Similarly, slipping off-post to visit family or going to a bar in town was a form of AWOL. An absentee would initially be charged with AWOL until the authorities could determine, either by the length of his absence or by discussions with his messmates, that he did not intend to come back. Once this had been established, he was declared a deserter. Desertion carried a minimum prison sentence and could, in extreme conditions (such as desertion in the face of the enemy), incur the death penalty.

Each company's dayroom had a log of men who had been given passes. Every soldier had to keep his pass on him and produce it upon demand. Any soldier walking through the front gate could be stopped by the MP on duty and asked to show his pass. Similarly, in town, MPs could stop soldiers and ask to see their passes. If a man could not produce his pass, he was arrested. Usually MPs did not stop soldiers unless the soldier was drunk, rowdy, or otherwise causing a public disturbance. Once a soldier was stopped, he was always asked for his pass.

Every unit had a mascot. The lady here is famous skater Sonja Henie, who was made an honorary colonel of the 508th at Frankfurt. Next to Henie is the unit commander, Col Roy Lindquist. They are standing in review, note the color bearer behind Lindquist's left arm. (Author's collection)

In barracks or town, men played poker and blackjack to pass the time. Others indulged in a variation of mumbly-peg. This dangerous game saw the soldier take his knife, holding it stabbing-style, blade down above the other hand with outstretched and separated fingers. He would then jab the point between each finger in sequence as fast as he could. The man who did it the fastest and the most times (without cutting off a digit) was the winner.

Classroom and hands-on training

Essentially there were two kinds of training classes in the military: classroom and hands-on. Classroom situations taught theory, hands-on concentrated on practical skills. The early weeks of basic training had a high PT (physical training) content, much of it in hour-long company calisthenics sessions. PT and drill occupied much of the new recruit's first weeks, sometimes up to half a day, every day. PT consisted of push-ups, running, chin-ups, jumping jacks, sit-ups, squat thrusts, four-count toe touches and rifle drill.

A formation of C-47s drops members of the 82nd Airborne. (Author's collection)

Calisthenics sessions, which were based around formalized physical activities, started with the men standing in formation, and shouting 'dress-right-dress!' to put distance between themselves and other soldiers. Once every soldier had his own personal space, exercise began. Sometimes, at the end of a set of exercises, soldiers were instructed to shout 'More PT, drill sergeant!' as if they really wanted it.

For a break in organized group PT, soldiers ran the company obstacle course or jogged five miles (8 km). Often small obstacle courses were set up outside the mess hall. These consisted of a run, dodge and jump, low crawl, chin-up bar, and overhead (monkey) bars. The run, dodge and jump comprised two waist-high barriers about one yard (91 cm) apart, which the runner stood in front of and, at a command, ran to one side of and between. Once the soldier was through the barriers, he jumped over a sand pit located one yard (91 cm) behind them. This part of the obstacle course taught agility, while the low crawl was good practice for crawling under machine-gun fire.

After the first few weeks of basic training, soldiers were placed on guard duty. This was a company duty and rotated among the training companies. Usually recruits guarded a supply building that was surrounded by a wire fence, or they walked a lonely post near office buildings. Rarely would recruits be entrusted with guarding a place of real responsibility. Often they walked a post in helmet and web gear, with a rifle and a fixed bayonet (usually in its sheath), but without ammunition.

At some point during the night the sergeant or corporal of the guard approached the post. He expected to be challenged with a cry of 'Who goes there?' The interloper would then give a counter-sign to identify himself and the guard would say, 'Advance and be recognized.' An eight-hour stand of guard duty at night, would typically be divided into two hours on, four off, and two more on, although it could vary. Some soldiers pulled four hours straight and then four off. The day after guard duty, men were tired, but they continued with their regular routine of training, learning to function despite sleep deprivation.

In the military, the term 'police' has nothing to do with the minions of the law (although there are Military Police). Police means to clean an outdoors area thoroughly, picking up paper, errant cigarette butts, and trash. In addition to guard duty, inductees could be put on Kitchen Police (KP), headquarters runner, dayroom duty with the NCO in charge, nightly fire detail, or hourly fire watch.

Kitchen Police was especially detested. Men on KP began work two hours earlier than other soldiers, they had to clean trays after meals, help prepare food for three meals (usually peeling potatoes and opening cans), and they were kept working until 2000 hours or even later. Their clothes and boots would be greasy and filthy, and they had barely an hour to get themselves ready for duty the next morning before lights out at 2100. Cooks, who were themselves under great time pressure, appeared more sadistic than other non-coms, and very few treated their charges with anything approaching civility.

Men assigned to fire detail kept the boilers running all night, stoking the furnace, emptying ashes into covered metal garbage cans, and watching so that the boiler didn't overheat. Fire watch was an hourly shift that rotated in the barracks, and each man caught it roughly once every ten days. Soldiers on fire watch were responsible for waking their relief and seeing that he was on duty before they turned in. After lights out, a man on fire detail patrolled around the barracks inside and out, checking that no fire had started from an errant cigarette butt, a hot ember from the hot water furnace, or arson. If he detected a fire, the fire watch was to wake his fellow recruits. All details prepared recruits for working on only a few hours sleep. A soldier's training had to teach him the realities of military life.

As 'basic' went on, training shifted from the PT-heavy instruction of the early weeks to more practical skills, such as the techniques of marksmanship, hand-to-hand combat, bayonet practice, grenade practice, and learning bivouac skills. The classroom studies, however, did not come to an end and always preceded the hands-on sessions.

Bivouac was frequently a city boy's first introduction to the great outdoors. This three-day event saw soldiers camp out, learning the basics of erecting a tent, digging a slit trench (latrine), walking guard duty at night, keeping an area secure, and protecting their weapons from night-prowling drill sergeants. Woe betide any man whose weapon disappeared, because the next day in formation, the drill sergeant would make an example of him. In addition to being browbeaten, the unfortunate recruit faced push-ups and extra duty

Paratroopers were taught rifle marksmanship in basic training and the use of special weapons in their subsequent individual training. Like every US foot soldier, the paratrooper was a rifleman first. Learning to fire a .45 caliber automatic pistol and to throw a grenade was also standard practice. The paratrooper followed bayonet training too, learning to thrust and slash, or even use his rifle stock in close combat.

During basic training, all soldiers learned unarmed hand-to-hand combat. Recruits were taught how to disarm an enemy who had a rifle,

The Airborne Center had a fixed cadre to train paratroopers who came through Jump School. These permanently assigned instructors stand in front of their unit sign at Fort Benning. (Airborne & Special Operations Museum, Ft. Bragg, NC)

how to fight with a knife, how to throw an enemy to the ground and stomp on him. No trick that could keep a US soldier alive was overlooked. Paratroopers were often given extra hand-to-hand training due to the nature of their combat missions.

After basic training, men were in good physical condition, understood the fundamentals of marksmanship, and were aware of the proper way to wear their uniforms. However, above all else, they had learnt how to obey orders. 'If I say jump,' the drill sergeant would say, 'I want you to ask "How high?".'

For a trainee paratrooper, 'basic' was just the first rung of a ladder. To climb to the top, a man would have to give his all and push himself to his mental and physical limits. Most soldiers would only discover those limits at Jump School.

JUMP SCHOOL

Paratrooper training, called Basic Airborne, is unofficially known as 'Jump School' and takes place at Fort Benning, Georgia. At Jump School, aspiring paratroopers learn how to pack their parachutes, how to ride properly in an aircraft, how to de-plane, how to fall safely past the plane's tail, how to open their chute and guide it to the ground, and how to rejoin their comrades to complete their mission. Paratroopers are trained not only to jump, land and fight behind enemy lines, but also to think, be resourceful, and complete a mission. During World War II, paratroopers could also take additional courses to enable them to become jumpmasters or pathfinders.

Jumpmasters were the on-plane experts who organized the jump. They were there to make decisions and solve problems, both on the ground and in the air. In training, jumpmasters were instructors, but in combat jumps, they were usually the officer or NCO at one end of the stick. Pathfinders were specially trained paratroopers who jumped into an area ahead of the main force and marked the drop zone, so that the aircraft could locate it. Sometimes pathfinders laid out landing zones (LZs) for gliders too.

AIRBORNE RECRUITS AND JUMP SCHOOL

Because paratroopers have to perform special tasks under extreme conditions, physical and psychological training is a must. Jumping from an airplane is easy the first time, but doing it again is much harder, because you know what's coming. The jump is physically quite straightforward, but the stress of the parachute yanking a falling soldier into a gentle descent is hard on the body. Landing is also perilous, and broken legs and sprained joints are commonplace. Cuts and bruises, as well as 'strawberries' (rough abrasions to the neck and sometimes shoulders from the chaffing of the harness) were the norm for the average World War II paratrooper. These were the acceptable risks of the job.

After basic training, soldiers knew that anyone with a stripe on their sleeve or bars on their collar was higher up in the chain of command and had to be obeyed. In the military, chain of command was usually all-important, but the airborne bent military protocol and further developed the individual. This was because of the nature of the paratrooper's job, whereby missions had to be completed at all costs.

A young sergeant on a training exercise at Lawson Field gathers his chute and wraps shrouds around it so that he can easily transport it back to the packing sheds after a practice jump. He wears a 1942-pattern jump suit and uses a T-5 camouflage-pattern parachute. (Airborne & Special Operations Museum, Ft. Bragg, NC)

Jump School lasted four weeks and was divided into four stages, which were labeled A, B, C, and D. Each stage was progressively more difficult than the former and each built upon the skills previously acquired. While the recruits went through Jump School, their cadre received additional individualized training in demolitions, ordnance, communications, or the like. Everything at Jump School was intended to prepare the paratrooper for a jump behind enemy lines.

The first week of Jump School (A stage) featured increasingly demanding physical exertion. Everyone ran everywhere, and when they weren't running, recruits were dropping and giving the instructor 20 push-ups. For fun, men ran the obstacle course outside the mess hall. While waiting for meals, soldiers were expected to stand at attention or run the obstacle course. No one ever walked, unless injured. It was an approach calculated to make or break the trainee.

The second week (B stage) saw a reduction in physical training and a growing focus on skills training. Men were taught the proper way to jump from an aircraft, how to guide the parachute, and

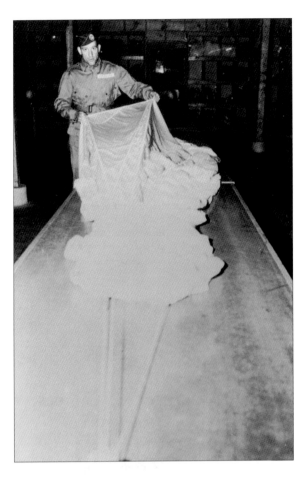

An instructor spreads out a chute in the packing shed, demonstrating to paratroopers the proper way to pack it. The shot bag just visible in the foreground holds the parachute lines straight and prevents them from tangling as the chute is packed. (Airborne & Special Operations Museum, Ft. Bragg, NC)

how to land. The paratrooper was familiarized with the key techniques that had to be mastered before he was ready for his basic mission. Paratroopers started by jumping from dummy doors just off the ground, graduating to sliding down controlled descent wires from 35-foot (16.5-m) towers.

Week three's training (C stage) taught soldiers the proper manner to pack a parachute in the packing sheds, how to leap from the 250-foot (76.2-m) jump towers, how to parachute free-fall, how to guide the parachute in practice, how to open the emergency chute, how to absorb landing impact, how to perform various rolls upon landing, and how to collect a chute and get to the staging area. Paratroopers may have initially lacked interest in the parachute packing hangars; however, eyes widened once the drill instructor mentioned that every man would jump using a chute he had packed himself. After that statement, interest in rigging and packing parachutes became intense.

In parachute packing sheds, parachutes were laid out on long tables before being packed, in reverse order, into the canvas covered metal-framed packs. Risers went in, then the shrouds, then the bottom of the parachute, and finally the apex, which was connected to the deployment bag and the static line. To keep everything separate and restrain the slippery silk, or nylon, chutes during packing, sausage-size bags of shot were laid across the chutes.

The last week (D stage) was the real thing: five jumps from aircraft – the last of which was a night jump. The height for the first jump was 1,200 feet (365 m); the second, 1,000 feet (304 m); the third and fourth, 800 feet (243 m); and the night jump 1,000 feet (304 m). After completing the night jump, a man was qualified to put on silver jump wings, blouse his pants into highly polished boots, and call himself a paratrooper. The final activity in Jump School was a formal parade, at which paratroopers were awarded their wings.

The basics of Jump School

Every paratrooper – from general down to private, from rifleman through chaplain, from medic to cook – went through Jump School and earned their wings. To earn wings, you had to jump and, at Jump School, your instructor was the law. Even officers going through Jump School had to obey their instructor's orders. With characteristic Airborne enthusiasm, instructors relished the task at hand. They would rarely speak in normal tones, opting instead either to bellow or to whisper. Most men preferred to hear bellowing as opposed to the barely constrained violence hidden behind the quiet voice of an annoyed instructor.

Raw recruits or those already in the military could request Jump School. Even officers had to volunteer. When asked why he became a

A sergeant steadies himself in front of one of the 250-foot (76.2-m) towers at Jump School. He is demonstrating the pull of an inflated chute, which can jerk a man off his feet, inflicting broken bones and sometimes causing death as it drags him along. Note the D-ring parachute release in his right hand. (Airborne & Special Operations Museum, Ft. Bragg, NC)

paratrooper the author's father replied, 'I was at OCS at Fort Benning. It was after lunch one day and before afternoon classes. The day was warm and I was looking at the sky, thinking how peaceful it was. I saw an airplane disgorge some paratroopers on a training exercise. They floated toward the ground. It looked serene, and I thought: "That's for me".'

The Airborne was a great experiment. Every soldier trained hard. It did not matter what a man was when he came to Jump School, what mattered was what he was when he left. A man wearing jump wings was self-reliant, a master of weapons, a team player, and believed the maxim: 'The difficult we do immediately; the impossible takes a little longer'.

Jump School routine

A standard day began with shaving and showering. This routine was followed by a five-mile (8-km) run before breakfast. After breakfast, soldiers quickly cleaned their barracks area for inspection, which occurred later in the morning, and then they fell in for classes. Sometimes classes were calisthenics or PT, while other classes taught skills such as parachute folding, proper landing technique (knees together, slightly flexed, ankles together, and toes slightly pointed to take up the impact of landing), and how/when to open the reserve chute. Practice sessions would see troops put on mock harnesses and learn how to guide the chute down a 35-ft (16.5-m) guide wire toward the ground. Troops were next introduced to the jump towers, from which they could experience mock-jumps. Men were raised 250 feet (76.2 m) into the air while wearing a harness that was released to give them the experience of free-fall and the shock of their chute opening (simulated by springs). Gradually the regime changed from strictly physical to the theory of jumping. The last week of Jump School was the final exam – jumping from an airplane.

The emphasis of Jump School was on physical and mental toughness. It was no shame to fall out on a run, but men were to complete the

In characteristic pose, this paratrooper grasps both sides of the C-47's doorway and is ready to jump. Hands at the door sides, foot on the lip of the doorway, he's ready to propel himself out of the doorway so that the next man, whose leg is just visible behind him, can jump. (Airborne & Special Operations Museum, Ft. Bragg, NC)

course, no matter how long it took. The Airborne wanted men who could do the task to which they were assigned, and they wanted men who would overcome any obstacle to do so. Drill sergeants made it easy for men to drop out, yelling: 'You want to quit, don't you? Tired of running? The infantry loves men like you, and *they* get to *walk* everywhere.' The message was clear: The Airborne was the best, and they wanted only the best.

General James M. Gavin once greeted a new officer by telling him what it meant to be an Airborne officer: 'That means you're last in the chow line and first out the door [as jumpmaster of the airplane].' If an officer expected maximum effort from his men, he had to match their commitment.

Long marches were common, and a 25-mile (40-km) hike in field gear was as much a part of training as a long-distance run. At the beginning of a run, the drill instructor might inform his charges that: 'we're going to run, and we're not coming back until ten men drop out'. The instructor would keep the run going until ten men were out of the formation. Only when man number ten had fallen out did the drill sergeant turn his formation back to the company area. Men who dropped out were expected to return to the barracks on their own.

2nd Lt Smith reminisced about one 25-mile (40-km) hike his platoon took in full field gear during summer: 'On the hike, we stopped after 15 miles and I pulled off my boots. I counted 14 blisters. I could see my men watching. Carefully I dried my feet and pulled my socks and boots back on my aching feet. Standing, I managed a small smile. "Your feet hurt. My feet hurt. When I drop out, you can drop out." Groaning, all arose and continued. Every man in my platoon completed the march. No other platoon managed that.'

Paratroopers learned to read maps, use a compass, and navigate to a designated location. Land navigation was an essential skill, because paratroopers were likely to land alone and need to quickly find their objective.

JUMP TOWERS AND FIRST JUMPS

Jump towers, with their steel crossbeams and protruding arms, look similar to modern power-line towers. They stand 250 feet (76 m) tall, and are square-sided with four arms (one for each side so that several students can use them at a time). This design also enables students to practice jumping regardless of prevailing winds. An office, supply room, or classroom is usually located between the legs of the base and the huge tower.

The trainee paratrooper is hoisted up in harness and dropped. A second later, when the springs stop the fall, the chute 'opens' with a jolt

Prior to 'saddling up', paratroopers on the runway staging area get a last-minute briefing before boarding an aircraft for a training mission. Only the jumpmaster (in the foreground) already wears his parachute. The paratroopers carry their musette bags as packs, and wear the light khaki 1942-issue jump suit with cinch belt, slant breast pockets. (Airborne & Special Operations Museum, Ft. Bragg, NC)

and the trainee has to guide the chute groundward in order to land properly. Every trainee had to follow this practice routine at least twice. On the way down, the drill instructor would yell instructions, for example, he might tell the jumper to change hands on his D-ring.

The final week of Jump School saw students make one jump per day for five days. Trainees were allowed to blouse their boots now, but only for the jumps. Back in camp, the boots were not worn bloused. A few men who completed every phase of school would discover that, when push came to shove, they couldn't jump. When the aircraft landed they were sent back to the company area and quickly transferred to another unit. Instructors at Jump School didn't want other paratroopers being exposed to men with a fear of heights. If a paratrooper was injured, he was sidelined until he was again fit for duty, and then he could complete Jump School. If for some reason he couldn't jump, he was transferred to another branch.

Taking the leap

Once the men saddled up (put on their chutes and harness), they formed sticks of 12 to 18 men (depending upon the size of the unit) and boarded the C-47s through the doors on the left side of the aircraft. These were the same doors through which the aspiring paratroopers would later jump. The plane flew them to the drop zone, and a red light turned green when the time was right for each man to jump. By the time the students reached the DZ, the aircraft's speed was 100 to 150 miles an hour (160 to 240 km/h). When the aircraft approached the DZ, the jumpmaster would stand. His parachute was a pilot's emergency, free-fall style chute, which did not connect to the static line.

The pre-jump check was governed by specific commands. As the plane approached its DZ, the jumpmaster would yell, 'stand up and hook up'. All paratroopers stood, faced the rear of the aircraft, and hooked up their static lines onto the cable. Next, the jumpmaster called, 'check equipment'. Each paratrooper checked his own gear, making sure every snap was snapped, every buckle buckled. Then the

Paratroopers watch for the DZ. The jumpmaster kneels by the door and the first member of the stick watches the ground below for identification panels or flares. The paratroopers clearly have some way to go before they reach the DZ, as the red light has not turned green. Only once the light has turned green will the men hook up. (Airborne & Special Operations Museum, Ft. Bragg, NC)

paratrooper checked the equipment of the paratrooper who stood in front of him. If mistakes were found, they were corrected. They told their partner his gear was OK.

Once the paratrooper's equipment had been checked, the jumpmaster bellowed, 'sound off'. This command meant that the men in the stick had to call out their number to confirm that their gear was in working order. The sound off started with the last man in the stick and went forward to the first man. Each man yelled out his number and then the word, 'OK'.

'Twelve, OK', '11, OK', 'ten, OK', and so forth until, 'One, OK'.

To number one, the jumpmaster called, 'Stand in the door.' To the remainder of the men in the stick, he yelled, 'Close it up tight', meaning they were to move toward the door where the first man waited. Ideally paratroopers should de-plane quickly, so that men from the same stick land in close proximity to one another.

The man at the doorway would grasp the doorway at ribcage height, putting his left foot on the door. The second paratrooper put his right foot against the first paratrooper's right foot, and his left behind the first man's left. This practice was followed until all men were closely positioned. At the signal (usually the jumpmaster tapping them on their left leg) the men would jump in sequence, each de-planing and turning left, toward the rear of the airplane, thus avoiding propwash and the accompanying thrust to the left

The jumpmaster would typically study the ground below, seeking signs that they were on course as they approached the DZ. Once he was satisfied that the mission was on course, he would shout 'Ready?'

'Yes,' everyone would chorus.

'Go!' came the next command, as the jumpmaster tapped the first man, who jumps immediately, turning rearward as he goes. The static line pays out, and then snaps taut as the paratrooper clears the rear of the C-47. While this happens, the next man steps to the door, the

jumpmaster taps his leg, and he exits the plane. Once training is complete, paratroopers usually follow at such close intervals that no taps are required. The stick moves forward, each man jumping in turn until only the jumpmaster and the static lines are in the door. Then the jumpmaster gathers the static lines, bringing them inside the aircraft for the ride home.

Once free of the plane, the paratrooper was taught to count, 'One-thousand-one, one-thousand-two, one-thousand-three...' as he fell. While falling at anywhere between 100 and 150 miles an hour (160 to 240 km/h), the static line ripped out the back of the pack and freed the chute and shroud lines. By the time the paratrooper reached 'one-thousand-three', his chute should have deployed. His plummet changing to a grinding halt when the canopy blossomed. Next, the paratrooper had to reach up and grasp his risers, ready to control his descent.

If for some reason there was no jerk by 'one-thousand-three', the paratrooper was supposed to look up and see if his chute was deployed. If it was, he was to see if it was filling with air, or if it was fouled. Sometimes chutes filled late. If the chute was fouled, the paratrooper had to lift his reserve chute with his left hand (so in deploying it wouldn't snap up and break his neck) and pull the reserve chute's D-ring with his right hand. In three more seconds the reserve chute should then open. Once the chute opened, the paratrooper was taught to see if there were any 'blown' (ripped out) panels that would change the dynamics of landing.

Sometimes chutes didn't open. The falling paratroopers and their chutes were called 'streamers'. The result of a streamer was often, but not always fatal.

Landing was by the book. Knees slightly flexed, legs together (not bicycling), toes down to absorb the impact, and ready to roll to help with the absorption. When the paratrooper hit the ground, he was to roll, get control of his chute, and collapse it. Once the chute was collapsed, the soldier was to get out of his harness, gather his chute, fastening it to the back of the pack-tray (using the bellyband), and then go to the assembly point. Once they reached their objective, those with serious injuries were put in ambulances and returned to the base hospital. The rest walked or limped back to camp.

For four days and one night, paratrooper trainees jumped. If a man's nerve failed, he was reassigned. If he was injured, he would have to make the remainder of his jumps when recovered. After five jumps, the man was a paratrooper and could pin the wings on his chest, and sew the paratrooper patch to his garrison cap.

Now he was ready for unit training.

Going overseas

Units developed their tactics and honed their combat skills while on maneuvers in the United States. The 82nd and 101st, for example, participated in maneuvers in Tennessee, having completed a period of training at Fort Bragg. One incident in Tennessee maneuvers foreshadowed some of the problems of D-Day. Paratroopers were practicing the British method of airdrops, in which aircraft flew line astern of the lead aircraft. Under this system, as each plane reached the

Nearly three sticks of paratroopers and parapacks filled with their gear are visible in this picture. The fully laden paratrooper in the foreground holds his forward risers, pulling down on them to maneuver his chute forward. (Airborne & Special Operations Museum, Ft. Bragg, NC)

DZ, the light came on, and the paratroopers jumped. American style saw the aircraft blanket the sky and paratroopers jump en masse. On the Tennessee maneuver, something in the line astern approach went wrong. The aircraft were astern, and the light came on. The paratroopers jumped and were scattered over more than 15 miles (24 km) of countryside. Some men spent more than four days returning to base.

After completing their training, paratroopers were granted a brief leave. They would return to camp, from where they were moved to a staging area. To maintain secrecy, most destinations and staging areas were kept quiet until the soldiers were en route. The paratroopers' addresses were APO (Army Post Office) numbers and these were at centralized areas on the West or East Coast. This precaution, which was supported by judicious censorship of outgoing mail, was intended to help maintain unit secrecy.

At staging areas (such as Camp Kilmer, New Jersey) paratroopers waited in camp (often with few, if any, passes) until their military transport vessel was ready to sail. When the vessel was ready, the men were moved dockside, shouldered their duffel bags, and boarded their transport (which would sail in secrecy), often linking up with convoys well offshore. These precautions were all taken to protect the transport vessels from U-boats. Casual conversations or idle references in letters, could easily divulge a unit's destination.

While on board the transport, soldiers were often limited to two meals per day – and even this was a monumental task for the messes aboard most ships. The men would spend their time doing calisthenics on deck, playing cards, reading, sleeping, or writing letters. They were rarely permitted to shower more than once on a typical ten-day voyage. If weather permitted, the men were allowed on deck, but if weather was foul, they were confined to their quarters below decks.

Living quarters were stuffy, and if the weather was rough, the number of seasick men grew geometrically due to the cramped conditions. There was barely room for two men to pass in the aisles between bunks, which were erected using metal water pipes and canvas. Storage for duffel bags and personal effects was located in the area between the bunks and next to the bulkhead. Often a paratrooper's duffel bag was so tightly crammed in that the owner could not access it for the duration of the trip.

A few units went directly to Africa, but most sailed for Europe. The Airborne's first port of call was Northern Ireland, where they established (and built) base camps and began to train. Camps were quickly set up, sometimes built from the ground up, and were usually located in the countryside (for reasons of secrecy and space). The paratroopers built the new bases along the lines of those at Fort Bragg and Fort Benning. These bases had wooden- or Quansett-hut structures, comprising barracks, day room, mess hall, and obstacle courses. Parachute-packing sheds, unit supply rooms, and motor pools were also set up.

With their base established, paratroopers returned to the regimen of classroom and maintenance training. Time was now spent on calisthenics, parachute packing, running the obstacle course, at the shooting range, on maneuvers in the countryside, and on everyday company duty. Life resumed in a comfortable rhythm, and often paratroopers were given passes for evenings or weekends.

Paratroopers with passes would eagerly descend on nearby towns and villages, attending community dances, visiting pubs, sampling local foods and beers, and seeing local sights. Most of the local areas endured rationing, but American soldiers had access to nylons, candy bars, and more meat. Often a gray area of commerce between locals and soldiers sprang up, and it was not uncommon to see locals with nylons or American cigarettes and Americans with Irish bacon or whiskey. In general, however, the often boisterous and fun-loving paratroopers rarely got into serious trouble with the people of Northern Ireland.

But the stay in Northern Ireland was only temporary. When the strategic thrust of the war became clearer, and men had acclimated to European weather, airborne units were transferred to England. The move took the paratroopers closer to mainland Europe and nearer to larger airbases. Here, airborne units underwent more training, more jumps, and more waiting.

Even in England, however, it still seemed that the war was far away, and that the Airborne would never get involved. When weekends came, paratroopers received passes and left their bases to meet their English cousins and see the countryside. As in Ireland, relations with the English populace were generally good, although American excesses often had conservative locals shaking their heads and protesting about US soldiers being: 'Overpaid, over-sexed, and over Here'.

Men from Raff's unit (the 501st), who had moved in with the 82nd, were treated as old hands because they had seen combat. These 'veterans' shared their knowledge with eager colleagues who had just arrived from the US. Paratroopers were impatient to find out when they would see action, but secrecy was the rule of the day. Men could only speculate, as they donned full gear for maneuvers or an alert, as to whether they were about to experience the 'real thing'. However, with the exception of the Italian Campaign, most paratroopers would have to continue to wait while the Allies finalized their D-Day planning.

This paratrooper private is in full jump gear with both chutes and field equipment. His weapons bag is worn on his left thigh, quick-draw style. This photograph was taken prior to a training exercise but, because no over-water flight is planned, the paratrooper does not wear a life vest. (Airborne & Special Operations Museum, Ft. Bragg, NC)

THE COMBAT JUMP

When a paratrooper boarded an aircraft, he was heavily laden. Usually a colleague had helped him to don his chute and gear before boarding. Once aboard the plane, some paratroopers knelt in the aisle with their loads resting in the seat.

In combat an officer jumped first, while the NCO was the last out. Once on the ground, the paratrooper gathered up his chute, bound it into his backpack using his bellyband and discarded it. The soldier then had to locate the rest of his stick. The officer and the NCO would move toward each other ('rolling up the stick') and would account for each man who had jumped. Most units had signs and countersigns to identify themselves to each other. Once all the men were accounted for, the stick began its mission.

ABOVE **This picture of Pvt Alonso, Co.B 508th, was taken while he was training in either England or Ireland. It shows him in class-A uniform outside his squad tent getting ready to go to a nearby town on a pass. He will wear a garrison cap with his uniform. (Author's collection)**

ABOVE, RIGHT **This photograph taken in England shows the officers and first sergeant of Co.B the 508th. Right to left: 1st Sgt Robert S. Gerald (KIA), 1st Lt Walter J. Ling (Bronze Star), Capt Royal Taylor (Bronze Star), 1st Lt Woodrow W. Millsap (Silver Star w/Oak Leaf Cluster), 1st Lt Carl Smith (Bronze Star). 1st Sgt Gerald wears the NCO class-A uniform while Ling wears officer class-As. 1st Lt Millsap has acquired an Army-Air Force leather jacket. 1st Lt Smith is dressed in the 1942-issue jump suit, the uniform which men of the 508th would wear on D-Day. (Author's collection)**

AIRBORNE EQUIPMENT

Early jump gear

Early paratroopers wore modified coveralls as jump suits and either cloth aviator's helmets or football helmets. The jump suit changed from standard army issue coveralls to silk coveralls for a short while, but the lightweight silk suits proved highly heat retentive. Coveralls were eventually abandoned in favor of the 1942-style lightweight tan drab jacket with slash breast pockets and cargo side pockets (plus a built-in belt) and baggy pants with multiple pockets, two of which were cargo-style and on the thighs.

At first regular boots and half boots were used, but these were replaced by the newly designed Corcoran jump boot. The Corcoran jump boot had reinforced leather toes and heels, which were made from separate rounded pieces of thick, saddle leather mounted on sturdy soles.

Early paratroopers jumped from B-18 bombers, but soon the Douglas C-47 became one of the most familiar sights in the war. This versatile and long-serving aircraft, which had a single cargo door on the left side (its cousin, the C-46, had a door on each side), was known to the military as the C-47 and to civilians as the DC-3. In early jumps, paratroopers were flown to drop zones by a dozen C-47 (Skytrain) aircraft. Each aircraft was capable of carrying up to 28 paratroopers and their equipment. The Waco CG-4A glider added to the Army Air Corps' delivery system. The Waco could carry six paratroopers and a jeep, light antitank gun, or field piece, or 15 glider infantrymen. Personnel entered through a door on the port side of the plywood glider and the nose swung up to allow a vehicle to be loaded.

THE PARACHUTES

The paratroopers of World War II used three primary parachutes: the T-4, T-5, and T-7, each chute replacing its predecessor. The T-10 parachute was issued after the war, and modified versions are still in use today.

The first parachute was the T-4, which was used by the Test Platoon and the original 501st at Fort Benning. It was in use in 1940 and opened with a static line. The visible differences between the T-4 and later versions were twofold. Firstly, the main chute was square and secured with three snap hooks, while the reserve chute was more rectangular and boxy. In this respect, the T-4 differed from the more lozenge-shaped later versions. Secondly, the T-4 was worn vertically on the chest and was bulky, leaving little room for additional equipment, whereas later reserve chutes were worn horizontally, thus providing space for extra gear. The T-4's harness was also looser than those on later reserve chutes. It was a cumbersome parachute that used space poorly, restricting the amount of gear a paratrooper could carry. The T-4's canopy deployed first, risers last.

In 1942 the 82nd Airborne was equipped with the T-5 parachute, reserve, and harness. When the T-5 was adopted, the parachute main pack had a bellyband that fed through the back of the reserve chute. It had a 'D-ring' with its handle to the right and was worn horizontally to the ground, thereby enabling other gear to be carried beneath it. The T-5, which had secure clips rather than a quick-release mechanism like that employed on British chutes throughout the war, was time-consuming to remove after landing. US officials felt that single-point quick-releases were dangerous, arguing that a paratrooper might inadvertently open the release, slide out of his harness while descending, and plummet to his death. Without a quick-release, the T-5 was safe, but cumbersome to remove. The T-7, which was introduced in 1944 and remained in use until the mid-1950s, was equipped with a quick-release mechanism.

The T-5 parachute was in use from 1942 until 1945. It opened with a static line, and had three snap-hooks. Each canopy panel consisted of four sections. The parachute had a wire frame-pack that was covered in canvas, and a harness that encircled the body. Like the T-4, its canopy

Fully loaded members of a stick en route to their DZ. The men relax as best they can while carrying a heavy load of field gear. They all face the rear of the aircraft, ready to stand, hook up, line up, and check the harness of the paratrooper ahead of them. (Airborne & Special Operations Museum, Ft. Bragg, NC)

Early paratroopers wearing T-4 parachutes with the reserve chute worn characteristically up and down. Both men wear cloth aviator helmets with chinstraps. The man on the left has half-boots and boot socks pulled over the legs of his pants. The man on the right has cinched the legs of his pants. Both paratroopers have their static lines secured over their right breasts. (Airborne & Special Operations Museum, Ft. Bragg, NC)

deployed first, risers last. The T-7 had four straps that met in the middle of the paratrooper's chest, one of which had a quick-release mechanism. As a safety feature, the quick-release dial was turned and a cotter key was inserted so that it could not be accidentally opened. The T-7's canopy deployed first, the risers last. To release himself, the paratrooper pulled the cotter pin and hit the center of the straps.

The paratrooper's issue parachute was colored olive drab camouflage with dark green, light green, and drab patches. The first parachutes were silk, but by the winter of 1943, they were being made from nylon. The harness and pack were cotton. All reserve chutes used by paratroopers were white. The chutes used by the regular Navy, Marines, and Army Air Force were white, as they were emergency rather than combat equipment. The parachute canopy has a diameter of 28 feet (8.5 m). An air vent (aperture) in the center is referred to as the apex, and the chute consists of 28 triangular panels that are larger at the bottom than the top. Suspension lines (shroud lines) run from the canopy to the risers and measure 22 feet (6.7 m) in length. Each panel has diagonal reinforcing bands that are sewn midway across the panel to prevent splits called 'blowouts'. A blowout makes the chute erratic and difficult to handle, causing a much faster descent than normal.

The parachute consists of several components: the metal-framed canvas backpack and webbed canvas body harness; the webbed canvas static line, ripcord and deployment bag; the silken shrouds attached to canvas risers, which connect to the harness; the shroud lines; and the parachute canopy. The paratrooper's chute is worn on his back, unlike a pilot's emergency chute, which is sat upon by the user.

The parachute harness can be visualized as an 'X' and provides a canvas saddle for the paratrooper. The shoulder straps extend from the backpack over each shoulder and continue down the front, looping around the back of the paratrooper's hips. The saddle is formed by the two straps that cross the parachutist's posterior. The straps come up between the legs at the upper thigh, connecting to the backpack at just below waist height, which explains why harnesses of this type are sometimes called 'nutcrackers'. Shoulder and thigh straps meet in a connector strap and lock-hook at sternum level across the chest. A bellyband, which is connected to the backpack, goes around the front of the paratrooper and buckles like a large belt on his left side.

The reserve chute fastens onto the bellyband horizontally across the paratrooper's stomach, and is deployed by a handle. All harnesses have adjustable belts and fixed tension buckles. Risers attach to the harness and feed into the packed parachutes. Two risers on each side connect to the harness near the paratrooper's shoulder. The top of the backpack is attached to the static line, becoming the deployment bag that rips off with the line when the paratrooper jumps.

Each panel of the parachute is reinforced with three diagonal silken cord braces. When a chute rips, reinforcement stops the split from continuing all the way up. Parachute suspension line cord (often called shroud lines by contemporaries) reinforces the edges of the chute. A total of 28 shroud lines connect the outer edges of the parachute to the risers. Each silken shroud is a woven silken sheath $\frac{3}{16}$ of an inch (4.7 mm) in diameter and surrounds a group of eight to 12 smaller silken cords, which are bundled inside for additional strength.

Shroud lines are evenly divided so that each of the four web risers has the same number of shrouds attached to it. Each riser connects to seven shroud lines. Web risers connect to the harness. There are two risers, which are arranged in a 'V' on each side of the parachutist's body. By pulling the risers, paratroopers can control the rate and direction of descent.

When the parachute is packed for use, only the body harness, the 15-foot (4.5-m) long static line and ripcord, and the backpack are visible. The canvas risers are folded first, then the shrouds are gathered and carefully combed (the lines are separated to avoid them tangling), and finally the chute canopy is folded and packed on top of the risers and shrouds. Once packed, the parachute backpack is laced up with ripcord lace. The laces are connected to the ripcord, which is connected to the static line. The static line is made from canvas web material and has a metal safety hook fastener on the end. This fastener hooks over a head-height, pencil-thick steel cable that runs the length of the aircraft's cargo bay. When a paratrooper de-planes, the static line pays out its length of 15 feet (4.5 m), and then jerks the ripcord, ripping the laces free to allow the deployment bag, chute, shrouds, and risers to pay out in the reverse order from which they were packed. After three seconds, the jumping paratrooper is below and behind the aircraft. When the chute opens, the paratrooper gets a huge jolt, but once deployed, descent slows to a more gentle float, providing the chute remains filled with air. The initial and violent jerk snaps teeth together and jolts the body of the jumper, digging the harness up into his crotch as his descent is arrested.

The paratrooper controls the direction and speed of his descent by spilling air from his chute. To spill air, he pulls on the appropriate riser. Sometimes parachutes fail to deploy properly, or the shrouds become tangled, or another paratrooper lands on the canopy and collapses it. Unless the paratrooper manages to fill his chute again, or deploy his reserve chute, he becomes a 'streamer'. Usually this is fatal, although a small handful of men have survived plummeting to earth.

PARATROOPER UNIFORMS

The first paratrooper uniform of significance was the 1942-style light-weight tan jump suit. This uniform consisted of a blouse with slanted breast pockets and expanding thigh pockets, a built-in belt, a special zippered neck pocket for the shroud-cutter switchblade, a concealed zipper, and double wrist buttons to adjust the cuffs of the sleeves. The jacket pockets were slanted down and toward the center of the jacket to give paratroopers better access while in a parachute harness or disengaging from the harness. The jump suit pants, which had cargo thigh pockets, were of the same tan lightweight material as the jacket.

An entire company floats toward the ground in an air drop during 1944. The paratroopers' chutes have all deployed and the aircraft are long gone. This drop was probably from more than 1,000 feet (305 m), judging from the height of the paratroopers and the lack of visible aircraft. (Author's collection)

1st Lt Carl Smith before D-Day. He is dressed in the 1942-issue jump suit and khaki garrison cap, but he does not wear 82nd shoulder patches. Note the gleam of the spit-shined Corcoran jump boots. On D-Day+1, Smith escorted more than 100 German prisoners who had been captured by the 508th, taking them back to the unit CP. (Author's collection)

During this post-war practice and demonstration jump at Jacksonville, a paratrooper demonstrates how easily it is for an inflated chute to drag a man along if it is not promptly deflated and rolled. (Author's collection)

This uniform saw service in Africa, Italy, and France. Many paratroopers on D-Day recalled that their uniforms were impregnated with a smelly chemical that was supposed to make them impervious to gas attack.

The 1942-style uniform was replaced by the 1943-issue. This heavier, darker green uniform was worn at Arnhem and Nijmegen. The 1943-issue was made from the same material as the regular army's fatigues and fatigue jackets, differing only in that the Airborne issue had cargo pockets on pants and jacket. Field jackets had a built-in drawstring around the waist in lieu of a belt, and had straight breast pockets. Because of its color and thickness, this uniform was better suited for Europe than the earlier issue.

By the jump at Operation Market Garden, all US paratroopers were wearing the 1943-style uniform. Many paratroopers had updated their uniforms when they were shipped back to England to train for Market Garden.

In his *History of the 508th Parachute Infantry*, William G. Lord II notes that, in addition to regular gear and weapons, many men of the 508th carried extra items in their voluminous pockets: '...One complete K ration, consisting of three meals, several D ration chocolate bars, two fragmentation grenades, one smoke grenade, one anti-tank Gammon grenade, and other articles...' could apparently be stowed in a paratrooper's pockets. The airplanes were as heavily laden as the men, and Lord notes that each C-47 carried '...six bundles containing light machine guns, mortars, ammunition, and mines. These were to be released by the jumpmaster just before he jumped.'

The earliest glider infantry, prior to World War II, wore the World War I issue 'dish'. Paratroopers, meanwhile, wore the cloth aviator's helmet to which goggles could be attached using snaps around the crown. After the aviator helmet was discontinued, paratroopers used American-football helmets, but the low rear neck and long ear protection were inefficient. Eventually, the paratroopers settled on the standard American army 'turtle' helmet, with only a chin-strap modification – the standard chin strap was replaced with an 'A' style chin strap and molded chin cup.

ABOVE **Taken on 30 November 1944, this photograph shows Tech Sgt 4th Grade Elek Hartman standing in front of his squad tent in a 1942-issue jump jacket. Hartman wears the garrison cap with his fatigue jacket. The Airborne circular patch, depicting glider and parachute, is on the left side of his garrison cap. (Author's collection)**

Jump School training, Ft Benning, Autumn 1942

A

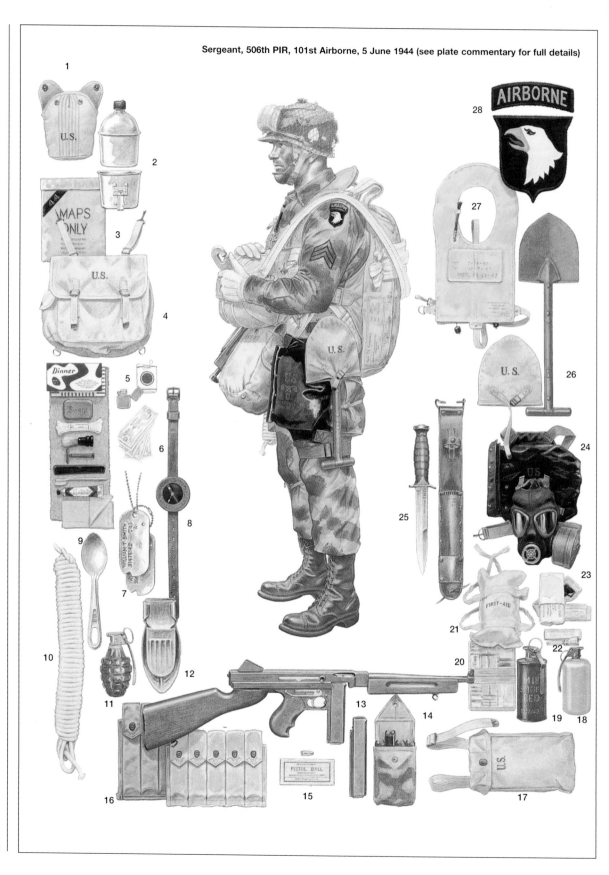

Sergeant, 506th PIR, 101st Airborne, 5 June 1944 (see plate commentary for full details)

B

Capt Frank Lillyman and Pathfinder Team A, 502nd Regt., 101st Airborne Division; St Germain-de-Varreville, Normandy, 0030hrs 6 June 1944.

C

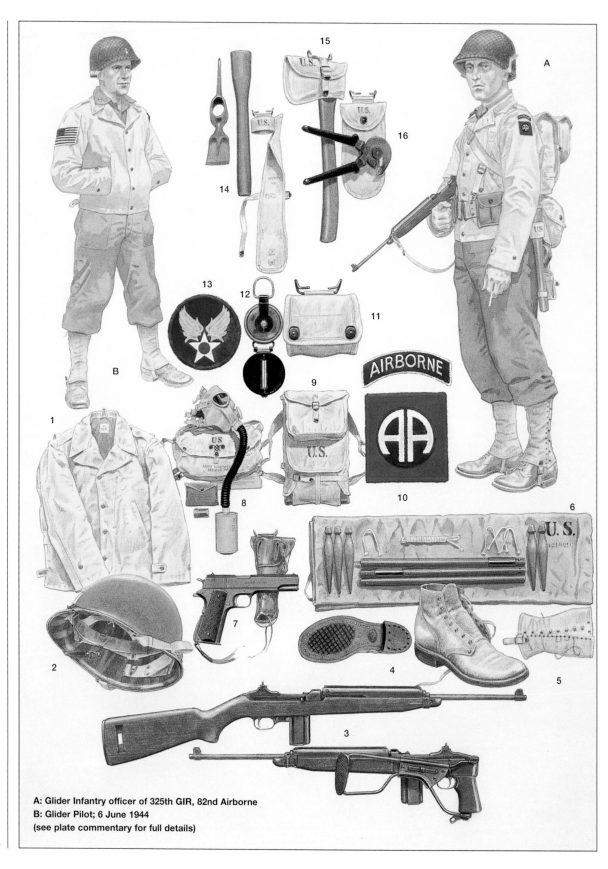

A: Glider Infantry officer of 325th GIR, 82nd Airborne
B: Glider Pilot; 6 June 1944
(see plate commentary for full details)

D

Paratrooper clothing
(see plate commentary for full details)

7

1

21

8

9

2

4

19

3

20

10

13

14

6

17

11

18

16

12

5

15

E

75 mm pack howitzer training, 457th Parachute Field Artillery Battalion; Camp Polk, Lousiana, February 1944

F

Demolition platoon paratrooper, 82nd Airborne: Operation Market Garden, 17 September 1944 (see plate commentary for full details)

Assault boats, 3D Battalion, 504th PIR; Waal River, The Netherlands, 20 September 1944

H

Tank hunter/killer team, 507th PIR; Wesel, Germany, March 1945

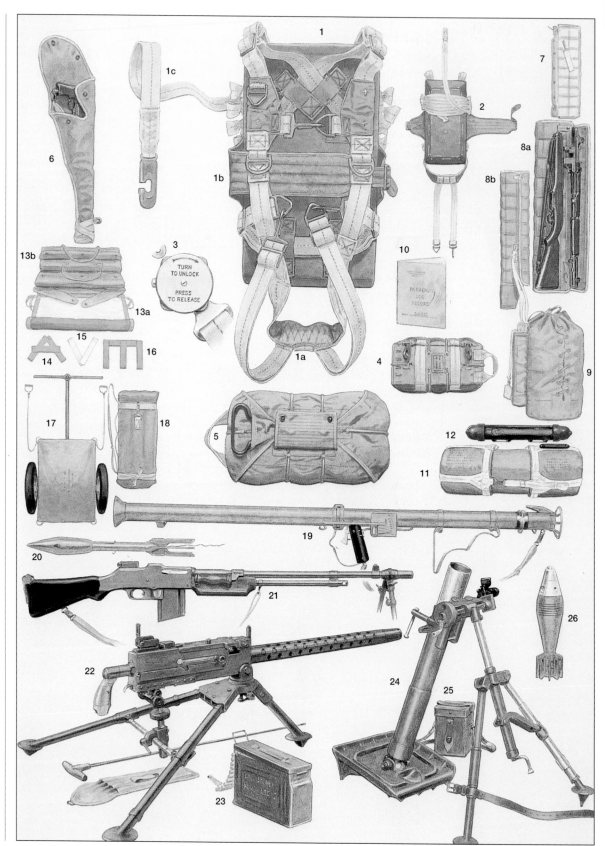

Jump equipment and team weapons (see plate commentary for full details)

Two paratroopers on maneuvers (perhaps in Tennessee) in mid-1944. Both men wear camouflaged coveralls and their web gear contains pouches for M1 charger clips. The flat ammo pouches are empty. The man on the left wears 'rough-out' combat boots, which had a two-buckle upper section and fewer laces than Corcoran boots. (Airborne & Special Operations Museum, Ft. Bragg, NC)

Perhaps the most distinctive paratrooper equipment (besides the parachute) was a pair of Corcoran jump boots. Jump boots had high tops, reinforced toes and heels, and were laced up tightly to provide ankle support for the jumper.

Extra issue items

A paratrooper was issued a compass, which was worn on the upper arm or as a wristwatch. He also had a shroud cutter switchblade to help him slice through entangling shrouds if he was caught in a tree. Shoulder arms were issued and, as with the US cavalry of the 1900s, early paratroopers were issued with pistols as sidearms. However, with units rapidly growing in size, by 1943 only 2,110 men of a division were armed with pistols.

PATHFINDER'S SPECIAL EQUIPMENT

Pathfinders were issued panel markers in bags so they could mark DZs in daylight. Special smoke grenades, Very pistols that fired colored flares, and radio transmitters that emitted a homing beacon for approaching aircraft to lock onto, were also issued.

GLIDER INFANTRY

Glider infantry, or 'Glider Riders' as they were popularly known, wore standard infantry equipment, including leggings. They did not receive jump pay and, unlike paratroopers, their fatigues and helmets were standard issue. They had regular infantry (not 'A-style') chin straps and did not use rifle bags (because they shouldered their rifles when they boarded a glider). At one time the rule of five jumps was relaxed so men could qualify for jump boots. This change did not meet with universal approval, and one Airborne company wag, who had no doubt worked hard to earn his jump boots, put a notice on a bulletin board stating that if anyone made one glider landing, he qualified to wear leggings.

WEAPONS

Paratroopers were issued with a number of weapons. The M1 Garand, a clip-fed .30-06 caliber semi-automatic rifle measuring 43½ inches (110.7 cm), weighs 9½ pounds (4.3 kg), has an effective range of 601 yards (550 m), holds eight rounds in an internal magazine fed by a charger clip, and fires as fast as the trigger can be pulled. The M1 features a bayonet lug under the barrel and has a metal butt plate. The M1 Carbine was semi-automatic only, and it was replaced by the M2 Carbine in 1942. The M2 is shorter than the M1 rifle (only 35½ inches [90.4 cm] in length), weighs 5½ pounds (2.5 kg), and has a range of 327 yards (300 m). The M2 was standardized in 1944 and saw limited use. It has a bayonet lug under the barrel and comes in either a full wooden stock version, or as the M1A1 (popularly known as the paratrooper version). This version, which is fitted with a folding 'skeleton' tubular shoulder stock behind the full pistol grip handle, was most frequently

This studio photograph shows a paratrooper wearing a camouflaged jungle coverall jump suit and parachute in T-5 harness. The shape of the distinctive paratrooper chinstrap is obvious, and from the caption, it appears that the paratrooper, who has completed his tour of duty, is set to be discharged. (Airborne & Special Operations Museum, Ft. Bragg, NC)

issued to Airborne engineers or artillery, rather than to Airborne infantry.

The Thompson M1 and M1A1 sub-machine-gun is 32 inches (81.3 cm) in length, weighs 10 pounds 5 oz (4.7 kg), and has a range of 109 yards (100 m). It operates on blowback, firing a .45 caliber cartridge from a straight 20-round (M1928A1) or 30-round (M1/M1A1 and M1928A1) box magazine, which is located beneath the bolt and behind the forestock. The bolt must be pulled to the rear to charge the weapon, which will then fire in either semi-automatic or full automatic mode, depending on the setting of the gun's selector switch. The M1928A1 has a detachable shoulder stock and a Cutts compensator on the barrel to offset the gun's tendency to climb upwards and to the right. The M1928A1 uses a 20-round box magazine or a 50-round drum magazine, which is heavy but tends to disengage because of its weight. However, by the middle of World War II, the M1 Thompson commonly used a 30-round straight magazine, had no Cutts compensator, and had a firmly attached shoulder stock.

The M3 and M3A1 'Grease Gun' sub-machine-guns are straight blowback, fully automatic weapons. They measure 29½ inches (75 cm) with their stocks extended, or 22½ inches (57 cm) with them folded. They weigh 7 pounds 15 oz (3.6 kg). The .45 caliber cartridges are fed from a 30-round box magazine (not interchangeable with the Thompson) located beneath the bolt. The Grease Gun features a pistol grip and a folding 'L' wire-stock. It fires only fully automatic, and a skilled gunner can fire in two- to three-round bursts. Its effective range is 109 yards (100 m).

The 1911A1 Colt .45 caliber semi-automatic pistol fires .45 ACP rounds, measures 8⅜ inches (21.8 cm) in length, weighs 2 pounds 7 oz (1.1 kg), has an effective range of 55 yards (50 m), and fires a single shot each time the pistol's trigger is pulled. It has a built-in safety grip in the butt grip, a seven-round magazine in the grip, and its slide must be pulled back to charge the first round. When the last round is fired, the slide locks in the open position to indicate the weapon is unloaded.

The Mk II and Mk IIA1 rifle and fragmentation grenade, 'Pineapple', holds two ounces (57 gm) of TNT, weighs 1 pound 5 oz (595 gm), consists of a fuze tube and grenade body. It can be thrown 33 yards (30 m), fired 154 yards (140 m) from a rifle and has an effective blast radius of 11 yards (10 m). The body is made of 30 square metal segments arranged in six rows of five, and is filled with an explosive charge. This charge causes the body to shatter when the powder explodes, throwing fragments in every direction. The fuze and primer handle is screwed into the body. A safety cotter pin, which holds the firing pin in a cocked position until the pin is pulled, prevents the striker handle from moving. To arm the grenade, the safety cotter pin is removed while holding down the handle. When thrown, the handle is flung away by the motion of the striker. The grenade's striker snaps forward (like a mousetrap) and the fuze primer is ignited, which in turn explodes the powder in the body, causing the grenade to shatter with the explosion. There is a presumed four to five second delay between the pin being pulled and the grenade exploding.

The M1 bayonet measures ten inches (25.4 cm) in length. It clips beneath the barrel of the rifle via a ring, which fits over the rifle barrel. The lower edge of the bayonet is sharp, and the first five inches (12.7 cm) of the reverse side is also sharpened. It can be used either as a hand-held knife or attached to the barrel of the rifle.

The Browning automatic rifle M1918A2 or BAR is a .30-06 caliber assault rifle. It measures 48 inches (122 cm), weighs 19 pounds (8.6 kg), and holds a magazine of 20 rounds. The BAR has two rates of automatic fire, 350 or 550 rounds per minute. It is a single man weapon and has an effective range of 880 yards (800 m), it can be shoulder-fired, or fixed to a bipod as a light-machine-gun. Airborne troops often removed the bipod to reduce weight and bulk.

The Browning .30 caliber M1919A4 light-machine-gun is a tripod or vehicle-mounted machine-gun with a 250-round belt. It measures 41 inches (104 cm), weighs 31 pounds (14 kg), and has an effective range of 990 yards (900 m). Early versions were liquid-cooled, but soon an air-cooled version became predominant. Generally, the gunner carried the gun and an ammo belt, while his assistant carried the tripod and two boxes of belted ammunition. Early World War II versions had a 250-round cloth belt, but later models used the 100-round disintegrating link belt, which made it possible to link large numbers of belts together. Although this weapon uses automatic fire, good gunners can shoot in three- to five-round bursts.

The Browning M2HB .50 caliber heavy-machine-gun is 57 inches (144.7 cm) in length, weighs 66 pounds (29.9 kg), has an effective 1,540-yard (1,400-m) range and has a carrying handle beneath the barrel. Early versions were water-cooled, but these gave way to air-cooled versions. It uses 100-round web or metal-link disintegrating belts. The .50 caliber round can penetrate light armor, soft-skinned vehicles, and is suitable for use as an antiaircraft weapon. Generally this weapon had a two-man crew (gunner and assistant gunner).

The 2.36-inch (6-cm) M1 antitank rocket launcher, or bazooka, was designed in 1918, but it was not introduced as a shoulder-fired, breech-loading weapon until mid-1942. The M1 launcher weighed 13.5 pounds (6.12 kg) and had a tube that was 54 inches (135 cm) long, which was fitted with wooden hand grips and shoulder stock. The weapon was electrically fired by two batteries in the grip, and it had a range of up to 300 yards (273 m). In the autumn of 1943, the M1A1 began to replace the M1. The M1A1 weighed 13 pounds (5.9 kg) and had a single handgrip. In October 1943, Airborne Command requested that the M9, which was fired by an impulse magneto in its handle, replace the M1 and M1A1. The M9's 5-foot (1.55-m) barrel could be broken into two sections while it was being carried or during parachute jumps The M9 had a 600-yard (545-m) range, a single pistol grip, and a metal shoulder rest. The M9A1, which incorporated an improved barrel coupling, soon followed and became the most widely used bazooka

The paratrooper on the left wears the late-war (1943-issue) jump suit and demonstrates how tie-down tapes can help support equipment and possessions carried in the paratrooper cargo pockets. His colleague wears the lighter 1942-issue uniform. (Author's collection)

This paratrooper in 1942-issue jump suit carries a folding stock M1 'Paratrooper' model carbine. He is on maneuvers at Fort Benning. Note the tall, scraggly Southern Pines and the hard, yellow Georgia sand and clay soil. (Airborne & Special Operations Museum, Ft. Bragg, NC)

model. The 2.36-inch (6-cm) M6-series high explosive antitank (HEAT) rockets could penetrate three inches (75 mm) of armor at 30 degrees impact and 4.5 inches (110 mm) at zero degrees.

The 2.36-inch (6-cm) bazookas, with a rate of fire of four to five rounds per minute, were the airborne infantryman's principal antitank weapons throughout World War II.

The 60-mm (2⅜-inch) M2 mortar consists of a tube, folding bipod, base plate (mount M2), and separate round. Muzzle-loaded, mortars could be moved and set up and then fired by dropping the round down the barrel, where it hit a firing pin and discharged. The 60-mm mortar fired 3.07-pound (1.39-kg) anti-personnel high explosive, 4.02-pound (1.82-kg) smoke, or 3.77-pound (1.71-kg) illumination rounds. Its tube measured 2 feet 4.5 inches (72.5 cm) in length, weighed 11 pounds 8 oz (5.21 kg), and had an effective range of 2,017 yards (1,837 m) for high-explosive (HE) rounds, 1,075 yards (977.27 m) for illumination rounds, and 1,610 yards (1,463.63 m) for smoke rounds. The M2 had a rate of fire of 18 to 20 rounds per minute. Plate, bipod and tube weighed 42 pounds (19 kg) in total.

The 81-mm M1 mortar is a smooth-bore, muzzle-loading, high-angle of fire weapon. It consists of a tube and base cap (containing the firing pin), bipod, and base plate. It weighs 44 pounds 8 oz (20.18 kg) and measures 9 feet 9 inches (2.97 m) in length. It fires light HE, heavy HE, illumination, and smoke rounds, whose respective ranges are 3,290 yards (2,990.9 m), 2,560 yards (2,327.27 m), 2,200 yards (2,000 m), and 2,431 yards (2,210 m). A standard light HE round weighs 7 pounds 4 oz (3.29 kg). The M1 has a rate of fire of 18 rounds per minute.

The 57-mm M1 and M2 antitank gun is a light, mobile, direct-fire infantry AT weapon. It is breechlock-loaded, has a vertical sliding wedge

Members of Co.B, 508th PIR, on parade in class-A uniforms at Frankfurt-am-Main in late June 1945. The men wear the white scarf and display their company guidon. Although the EMs and NCOs wear OD class-As, the officers wear the dark OD 1943 jacket and 'pinks' (light gray-beige) slacks bloused into their highly polished Corcoran jump boots. (Author's collection)

breechlock, and is capable of penetrating medium armor. The M2 has a caster on its right trail, and features different handspike, utility box, rammer brackets, shield apron hooks, trail handles and spreader than the M1. Mounted on a two-wheel, single axle carriage, the M2 has a low center of gravity and weighs 2,700 pounds (1,224.5 kg). Artillerymen can emplace it in 90 seconds. It fires a 13.73-pound (6.22-kg) APC-T round to a range of 13,556 yards (12,323.63 m). It can also fire a 12.8-pound (5.8 kg) HE-T round to a range of 12,670 yards (11,518.18 m).

The 75-mm M1A1 pack howitzer is a carriage borne, single shot artillery piece. It has a wedge, horizontal sliding, hand-operated breech. The M1A1 measures 12.08 feet (3.68 m) in length and weighs 1,440 pounds (653 kg). It has a range of 9,610 yards (8,787 m)for HE and WP smoke rounds, and 7,000 yards (6,363.36 m) for HEAT rounds. The M1A1 was regarded as a good infantry field piece, having a rate of fire of 140 rounds per hour. Six artillerymen could, when no gun tractor or truck was available, manually pull the M1A1 by the trails over ground. Although the M1A1 is lighter and has a longer range than the 105-mm M3, the latter has more punch than the 75-mm gun.

The 105-mm M3 pack howitzer is a carriage borne, single shot artillery piece that has a wedge, horizontal sliding, hand-operated breech. It measures 19 feet 8 inches (6 m) in length, weighs 4,475 pounds (2,029.47 kg) and has a range of 12,150 yards (11,045.45 m) for smoke or HE rounds, and 8,959 yards (8,144.54 m) for HEAT rounds. Hydro-pneumatic recoil and manual operation, plus a 100 round per hour rate of fire, make the 105-mm M3 an ideal infantry support weapon. A snub-nosed version, which was delivered by glider, has a shorter range than the 75-mm gun, but uses a heavier shell that compensates in hitting power. When glider troops land, the regular barrel 105-mm guns are brought in to reinforce the paratroop artillery units.

As these paratroopers jump, the parapacks under the wings of their plane are released. The jumper's static line has pulled his deployment bag loose and his chute is starting to come out of his pack tray. A second paratrooper has jumped from the doorway and a third is poised in the door, ready to go on command. (Airborne & Special Operations Museum, Ft. Bragg, NC)

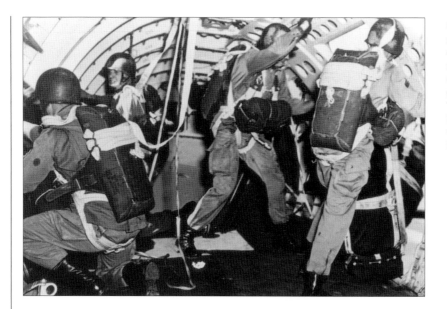

THE PARATROOPER IN COMBAT

The Pathfinder

The Pathfinder went ahead and found the way for those who followed. Pathfinders had to make the DZ visible to the paratroop and glider units that followed them on a mission, but, while doing this, they had to remain hidden from the enemy. To help them in their task, Pathfinders were issued with four essential pieces of equipment: low-tech ground identification panels (which were large, colored sheets of fabric carried in a self-contained OD bag); high-tech Krypton lights; 5G radio transmitters; and Eureka radar devices to help aircraft locate landing sites. At Sicily, the 5Gs were not used. In transit one of the 5Gs had broken loose and smashed; consequently, the Pathfinders had little faith in them and so did not use them. The Eureka radar sets were operational within three minutes. As a back-up, Pathfinders had colored flares, which were fired from Very pistols, to identify general areas for approaching aircraft. In daylight, pilots would see the ground panels marking the DZ.

Once landed, the Pathfinder hid his parachute, assembled his gear and weapon, and moved to the DZ. At Sicily, two of three Pathfinder groups dropped on target. On D-Day, many Pathfinders dropped in flooded fields, were captured, or were well off-course. Nevertheless, the efforts of those in the right place helped harried troop-carrier pilots locate their DZs.

PARATROOPERS

The most frequent mission directive given to paratroopers was to: 'Disrupt enemy communications, delay enemy reinforcements, and accomplish mission.' Paratroopers approached missions with a 'can-do' attitude, but getting to where they were supposed to be was not always easy. Jumping from an aircraft is not necessarily a matter of pinpoint accuracy. On D-Day,

Mixed 504th and 508th Pathfinders in plane number 16 (5 June 1944). Soldier reclining is unknown. Seated (left to right): Pfc Nicholas Trevino (wounded, evacuated); unknown of 504th; unknown; Pfc Cipriano Gamez (Bronze Star); unknown; Pfc Demciak; Pfc Donald E. Krause (WIA, Bronze Star). Kneeling: Pfc Wilburn L. Stutler (Bronze Star); Pfc J.T. Barkley (Bronze Star); unknown; Pvt James H. Weinerth (Bronze Star, w/Oak Leaf Cluster); unknown; Pvt A.B. Cannon (Bronze Star). Standing: Gilliam (air crew); Wilger (co-pilot); unknown (504th); Cpl R.J. Smith (Bronze Star); Herro (navigator); unknown (air crew); Miles (pilot); 2nd Lt Weaver (killed in action). Soldier in door unknown (air crew). (508th PIR Museum, Camp Blanding, FL)

things went wrong for many paratroop units, including the 508th. William G. Lord said: 'A quick hopeful glance at the terrain below was enough to tell most of the Regiment that they were not in the proper place, but were lost several miles into enemy territory.'

On the first day's drop over Italy, 'friendly fire' would account for several Allied planes, a number of gliders, and many lives lost. The next day, and despite warnings from the top, the same thing happened to paratroopers who were struck by naval gunners who had become nervous from constant Luftwaffe attack. Thereafter, paratroopers approached a DZ tentatively, aware of the perils inherent in their mission. No matter how nonchalant a paratrooper appeared, all were concerned about the jump.

Because of the threat of enemy antiaircraft fire, some jumpmasters had their men hook up 20 to 30 miles (32 to 48 km) from the drop zone. This practice meant that, if the plane was hit, the men would still have a chance to jump. Captain Royal Taylor of the 508th PIR had his men hook up when they reached the English Channel.

More than one paratrooper spoke of how agonizing it felt to stand, poised in the doorway, as tracer rounds zipped nearby. It was almost as helpless a feeling as that experienced by the soldier as he floated down under enemy fire, with only a disassembled and unloaded weapon to protect himself.

On the ground, the paratrooper had to assemble his weapon, locate other members of his stick, orient himself, and then fulfill his mission.

Pathfinders in plane number 17 (5 June 1944). Seated (left to right): 2nd Lt Perez (air crew); 2nd Lt Vohs (air crew); 2nd Lt E.F. Hamilton (KIA, Bronze Star); 1st Lt Gaudion (pilot); 2nd Lt L.L. Polette Jr. (KIA, Silver Star w/Oak Leaf Cluster); unknown (air crew); unknown (air crew). Kneeling: Sgt Katsanis (504th); Pvt Howard Jessup (later awarded a Bronze Star); Pvt R.L. Seale (Bronze Star); Cpl Ernest King (KIA); Pvt Frederick J. Infanger (Co.E, Bronze Star); Pfc Murray E. Daly (Co.D, KIA, Bronze Star); Pvt John P. Perdue (Co.D, KIA); Pfc Carl W. Jones (KIA). Standing: Pvt Mesenbrink (Bronze Star); Pvt Robert A. Andreas (Co.E, Bronze Star); Pvt John G. Gerard (Bronze Star); Pfc Beverly J. Moss (Bronze Star); Pvt Norman C. Willis (Co.E, Bronze Star); Pvt Forkapa (504th); unknown (504th); unknown (504th). Soldier in door is 2nd Lt Murphy (504th). (508th PIR Museum, Camp Blanding, FL)

The compass was now his most important piece of equipment. Paratroopers had to move unseen, treating everyone as a direct information conduit to the enemy. Moving quickly but stealthily, the paratrooper kept his head down and his rifle ready. With luck, an officer or NCO would be moving toward him, collecting members of the unit so that they could complete their mission. Wallace Swanson of the 502nd PIR recalled his landing for Gerald Astor: 'I landed in three or four inches of water covering a grassy area. My chute collapsed. I collected it and hid it.'

Landing at D-Day, 1st Lt Barry E. Albright of Co.E, 508th PIR recalled his experiences: 'A burp gun was firing from the far hedgerow... It took... twenty minutes to work myself out of my chute.' Albright added, 'It was quite clear that we could not assemble and secure our equipment as planned... (so) I figured the direction most likely to lead to the battalion defensive area. At five in the morning I found the Battalion CP.' Some paratroopers landed and acted with caution, while others displayed bravado. During the Battle of the Bulge, when told his unit was cut off and surrounded by superior German forces, one paratrooper quipped: 'The Germans have us surrounded – the poor bastards!'

There were instances during World War II when paratroopers fought as regular infantry (i.e., without having first been dropped into battle, or participated in an amphibious landing), however this was not the norm. The advantage of a sea landing was that equipment and supplies were more likely to reach the area where they were needed. In the case of an airdrop, it was not uncommon for supplies to be lost and never found.

Like all dropped supplies, medical supplies were at the whim of wind and man. Corporal George Moore of 3rd Battalion/508th was at an aid station and observed a badly wounded soldier. 'There was no plasma or

This photograph shows a classic Airborne landing. Most of the paratroopers have just hit the ground and are rolling or trying to get up. Note the stance of the paratroopers who have not yet touched down – 'legs together and knees slightly bent'. (Airborne & Special Operations Museum, Ft. Bragg, NC)

morphine,' recounted Moore. The soldier whose legs were badly injured cried out: 'Oh God, please let me die...' Paratroopers were taught basic first aid and many carried extra compresses on their helmets. A compress was placed over a wound, sterile side down, and pressure applied to stop or slow the bleeding. The paratrooper then yelled for a medic and continued his mission.

The wounded were patched up where possible, or evacuated if their injuries were serious. Some wounded were captured, patched up, and then sent to POW camps. Others were taken to the rear by medics, loaded on boats or LSIs and returned to England to convalesce. When healed, paratroopers were either returned home for discharge, or sent back to their unit's depot so they could rejoin it.

Once free of his parachute, the paratrooper pulled his M1 from its Griswold bag, assembled it, and then loaded it. Those jumping with M1 carbines clipped the stock open, slammed a magazine in the weapon, and charged it. Some men using magazine-fed weapons (e.g., the Thompson) taped two magazines together. That way, if surprised while struggling out of his gear, the paratrooper had 40 rounds that he could quick-load and fire.

Over Ste. Mere Eglise, Capt Royal Taylor released parapacks of the 508th's equipment and jumped. Taylor was slightly injured on landing, and quite a few paratroopers (from a mix of units) landed in trees, or on telephone poles. A few dropped very low, while some were so heavily laden with items in their pockets that, when their chutes opened, their pocket seams ripped open and items were lost. A few jumpers drifted helplessly into burning buildings, their ammunition and grenades exploding in the flames. Ground forces shot down men who descended over German

As revealed by the smiling faces of the medics (their helmets are marked with a white circle around a red cross medical symbol), these men at Jump School have landed without mishap. In combat, medics might also wear a brassard to further identify themselves. The medics in this picture are dressed in 1942-issue uniforms and medical webgear harness. The lieutenant (in the foreground) sits on a parachute canopy. The technical sergeant (left) wears the shoulder patch of the Headquarters Airborne Center Training Detachment. (Airborne & Special Operations Museum, Ft. Bragg, NC)

positions and many paratroopers saw friends killed as they dangled like targets in their harnesses. Paratroopers who survived learned, and in the daylight drop in the Arnhem-Nijmegen-Eindhoven campaign, they jumped with loaded weapons so they could come down blazing.

Inevitably, on D-Day, men were a mélange from different units, all with separate missions and each trying to find other members of their units. In the darkness, men mistook each other, lost maps and valuable equipment in flooded fields, and became disoriented. For a unit to land together, they had to jump in close proximity, nobody could hesitate at the door, they had to avoid antiaircraft and ground fire, and the pilot had to maintain a steady course. The potential for chaos was immense.

Tired from hours of waiting and the stress of the jump, some paratroopers froze when they hit the ground. S.L.A. Marshall, who was trapped in hedgerows by German fire on D-Day, recounts that 1st Lt Woodrow Millsap of the 508th told his men: 'Keep moving till we close on them. Hold your fire till I give the word.' The men followed until a German machine-gun opened fire but, startled by enemy fire, his men went to ground. Seeing enemy fire kicking up dirt, Millsap bulled his way through the hedgerow, shouting for his men to follow. No one did. They weren't terrified, just tired and under stress. 'What's the matter... no guts?' he yelled. No one budged until another officer came along and helped Millsap move them out.

On D-Day, landings were unpredictable, often putting mismatched groups of men in proximity. General Maxwell Taylor landed in an area where several men gathered, most of them officers and only two or three enlisted men. Recalling the incident for Cornelius Ryan, he quipped, 'Never have so few been commanded by so many.'

GLIDER TROOPERS

If jumping from an aircraft required courage so too did crash landing in a glider made from plywood and metal. Parachute field artillery and glider field artillery units had to crash land in enemy territory, which was often bestrewn with potentially lethal telephone poles, before assembling their personnel and weapons, including their field piece. Vic Warriner told Gerald Astor of his glider's landing on D-Day: 'The crash was only minimal. The Plexiglas stopped falling... and all I got out of the experience was skinned knees.'

In theory, glider artillerymen clambered out of their gliders and immediately set up their guns. However, in practice, they would often have to spend valuable time locating their weapon before they could do anything. Taking a 75-mm howitzer's components out of parapacks and putting the pieces together was simple, unless of course the parapacks were lost. Once the field piece had been assembled, men then had to find rounds for the gun. With gun and ammunition ready for action, the gun crew had to orient itself and move to a designated support position.

Glider artillerymen were also hit hard if their cargo tore loose en route. After D-Day, more than one glider was found with its crew dead, having been crushed by vehicles and cargo upon impact.

ON THE GROUND

Paratroop landings are frequently chaotic. During World War II, many pilots dropped their men low. According to some paratroopers, the planes delivering the 508th were as low as 500 feet (152 m) off the ground. Jump time was cut down to three seconds for the chute to open and five or six seconds until touch down. Men were scattered over dozens of hedgerows. 1st Lt Carl Smith recalled: 'I think we jumped at what seemed like 800 feet. It was low. In the dark, I could see lights and both small-arm and antiaircraft fire before I touched down. I landed in a tree that was in a field surrounded by hedgerows and I had a time trying to get my knife out to cut my risers. When they parted, I fell about 20 feet, and a rotten log broke my fall. Once out of the hedgerow, I couldn't locate my men. I kept moving from hedgerow to hedgerow. I linked up with a sergeant from another unit, and we spent most of the day moving toward our objective where we heard firing. Toward the end of the day he was killed by enemy fire. That evening I made contact with the rest of the 508th'.

S/Sgt Harrison Summers of Co.B, 502nd PIR with the 101st landed near Ste. Martin de Varreville. His mission was Objective W, where there were four 122-mm antiaircraft guns in bunkers. Objective W was within one mile (1.6 km) of Mesieres, west of Ste. Martin de Varreville. An 11-building farm complex (known as XYZ Complex) provided lodgings for the German antiaircraft batteries, and this became the immediate

objective for S/Sgt Summers' hotchpotch platoon. Summers' troops had been assembled from other units and, somewhat predictably, the men did not work well together. The men were reluctant to assault the objective, so Summers decided to lead by example, taking on the first of the 11 farmhouses alone.

Summers found himself backed by several of his troops for the second assault, and he methodically attacked each farmhouse in order. At building 11 (which was occupied by 80 German soldiers), S/Sgt Roy Nickrent came forward with a bazooka and put several rockets into the upper story and roof. Faced with Nickrent's bazooka and Summers' steady advance, the Germans abandoned the building and fled. Well before supper, Summers had cleared all the buildings, routing over 100 German antiaircraft troops and killing 20 of them.

Wearily, Summers sat and smoked a cigarette after taking building 11. When asked why he had staged his one-man combat assault, he drew on his cigarette and replied: 'I have no idea why I did that,' adding, 'I wouldn't do it again under the same circumstances.' Perhaps it had been the instinctive act of a courageous man, or perhaps it had been the product of intense and specialized training. The important thing, however, was that the mission had been accomplished.

Company B of the 508th PIR was an average unit with an average story to tell. They jumped into Europe at strength. However, when they left, their day report showed 148 officers, NCOs, and enlisted men accounted for by 9 July 1944. The report shows that 18 were KIA (killed in action, 12 per cent), 24 were MIA (missing in action, 16 per cent), 48 were WE (wounded-evacuated, 33 per cent), 47 (33 per cent) present, and 11 (six per cent) were transferred. Two of the unit's sergeants received battlefield commissions to lieutenant. The casualty rate for D-Day to D+35 included KIA, MIA, and WE, but at 61 per cent manpower loss (Eisenhower had anticipated losing 85 per cent or even 100 per cent) the Airborne's mission was a success.

During the Sicilian campaign, Gen Ridgeway's men were scattered all over the map, far from the DZ. Ridgeway was determined to find them and decided to assess the situation firsthand. He took what he described as 'the loneliest walk' of his life, walking toward where he thought his men should have landed. Ridgeway moved into enemy territory and gathered together 20 men, all of whom were disoriented and confused. Ridgeway was so upset by the scattering of his men that he returned to American lines and advised Gen Patton to cancel a planned drop of the 504th.

Gen Gavin was among the missing during the Sicilian campaign. He had landed more than 25 miles away from the DZ and found himself among only 20 men, many of whom (including his S-1 and S-3) were injured. After much contemplation, Gavin decided to start moving toward the sound of the guns. All but six men fell out. Crossing a ridgeline they came under enemy fire, which downed one man. Gavin's men returned fire, but their carbines jammed. As the volume of enemy fire intensified, Gavin realized that his five men were up against a platoon. They withdrew during an enemy mortar barrage.

While hiding in a ditch Gavin fumed about jammed weapons, and about the scattering of his carefully trained men. He felt helpless. On the second day he encountered a friendly outpost and learned that he was still 15 miles (24 km) off course. As they crossed through German lines on their way to safety, Gavin's men followed standard paratrooper practice and cut telephone lines to disrupt enemy communications.

In similarly chaotic circumstances, Gen Gavin arrived at Biazza Ridge. However, this time he found around 250 US paratroops from the 3rd Battalion and quickly assembled them into an ad hoc unit to hold positions and fight German probing units in the area. Gavin's unit achieved great success and forced enemy probes back. The Germans responded in emphatic fashion, sending an armored column against the paratroopers.

The 505th PIR was on its own, and some of the heaviest fighting of the Sicilian Campaign ensued. Lightly armed paratroopers with bazookas and squad weapons held the ridge line tenaciously. Mortar fire began walking down the line of paratroopers who were furiously digging in. The paratroopers fired their bazookas on German tanks at close range, but saw their projectiles bounce off. The tanks quickly began to overrun the 505th's shallow foxholes. The paratroopers did enjoy some success against the German tanks by firing their bazookas into the tank's soft underbelly, which was exposed when it cleared small elevations. However, squad weapons against armored fighting vehicles is an uneven match.

Despite their lack of firepower, Gavin was determined that his men should hold their ground. He told the 505th unit commander that they '...were going to stay...(on)...the ridge with what we had and fight the German infantry that came with the tanks'. The 505th held Biazza Ridge and were soon supported by a battalion of the 45th Infantry Division. Back-up continued to arrive, this time in the shape of the 456th Parachute Artillery's 75-mm howitzers. With a few pulled strings, naval fire from cruisers and destroyers against the German positions was also forthcoming.

As naval salvos started blowing up fields, Gavin felt that the tone of the battle 'seemed to change'. The ferocity of the German attacks lessened and Gavin realized that it was the perfect time for a German counter-attack. He rounded up his men, much as Patton would do at Bulge, armed them, and charged down the hill into German lines. It was the last thing that the Germans expected and they were routed.

Front (top) and rear views of a Safe Conduct pass that was issued by the 508th PIR to captured German soldiers. The terms of surrender attested to by Gen Eisenhower's signature at the bottom included: disarming the soldier, treating him well, feeding him, removing him from the combat area, and giving medical treatment if necessary. (Author's collection)

Members of the 508th PIR load German prisoners aboard a train for transfer to a rear area during early 1945. The American soldiers with white stripes on the rear of their helmets are officers. (Author's collection)

Ridgeway felt that this was the turning point in the campaign for Sicily. For his actions, Gen James Gavin was awarded a Distinguished Service Cross. Other men fought no less heroically. In *Currahee* Donald R. Burgett tells of an American lieutenant who started across a field when bullets began spurting in the dust around his feet. The lieutenant returned to where his 17 men lay and told them: 'This town is a German fortress...you can see catwalks in the treetops.' When asked what his plan was, he responded: 'A head-on attack, and the sooner the better'. After a hard fight, the Germans began withdrawing. Upon taking the town, the Americans learned from a prisoner that over 200 Germans had been positioned there. When asked why the Germans had pulled out, the prisoner said that they thought: 'the whole invasion was directed right at them and never dreamed that only 20 men armed with rifles would attack over 200 well-armed soldiers in stone fortifications.'

Sometimes, a paratrooper's best course of action was to play dead. As Pvt John Steele of the 505th PIR floated toward Ste. Mere Eglise's town square under intense enemy fire, he saw one man go limp in his risers and another explode when munitions he carried were hit. Pvt Steele was himself hit and, as a numbing pain shot through his foot, he collided with the town church. His chute collapsed as he slid down the roof of the church and over its side. Steele came to a halt on the church's eaves, dangling just above a maelstrom of German soldiers who were firing at the paratroopers. Struggling, he reached for his knife, but it slipped from his fingers. Steele was trapped. He closed his eyes and hung limp, giving the impression of a dead paratrooper hanging from his risers. Several hours later, German soldiers discovered that he was alive, and cut him down.

Gradually units converged on pre-set areas, or were directed to where their unit was re-forming. All this occurred behind enemy lines while ground forces tried to link up with the paratroopers. Paratroopers destroyed communications, controlled vital roads, drained off enemy reserves needed elsewhere, and captured key positions such as radio stations, radar emplacements, crossroads, or bridges. Although their landings had been far from perfect, they had created chaos for the enemy.

The 508th PIR parade as guards to Gen Eisenhower in June 1945. Every man in their color guard wears a full helmet, rather than a helmet liner, and all are dressed in class-A uniforms with service ribbons. Some soldiers carry rifles, but they have no ammunition pouches on their web belts. (Author's collection)

Sometimes paratroopers fought as line infantry. When the German Ardennes offensive caught the Allies by surprise, troops dug in and toughed it out. Fortunately for the Allies, American paratroopers met some of the offensive. These men, who had been trained to fight far from support, were confident and self-assured. As the 101st stood surrounded at Bastogne, Gen MacAuliffe famously replied, 'Nuts!' to a German demand for surrender.

Meanwhile the 82nd drew a line about 12 miles (19 km) behind Bastogne and five miles (8 km) in front of Malmedy. US armor was moving heavily through the snow, in an effort to stop the oncoming German panzers. Gerald Devlin recounts an incident at Manhay when an armored column saw a paratrooper bazooka-crew manning a snow-covered bunker. 'Where are the American lines?' the commander yelled to the gunner. Pfc Thomas Martin of the 325th GIR (of the 82nd) stood and indicated the area behind him. 'Pull your tank up behind me,' said Martin, 'I'm the 82nd Airborne Division, and this is as far as the bastards are going.'

It was not only airborne foot soldiers, but also commanders that were given to flirting with danger. Gen Ridgeway, for example, had a reputation for hopping in his Jeep, having his driver go forward, and then getting out to take a look around. In his Jeep he carried his .30-06 Springfield rifle as a personal weapon, which he kept loaded with armor-piercing ammunition.

On one such jaunt, at Bulge, Ridgeway got out of the Jeep and took off through the snowy woods with no support. Clay Blair relates that Ridgeway 'heard a tremendous clatter' between him and his Jeep. He turned to see a German AFV crossing the area that he had just moved through. Ridgeway began shooting and sent five shots through the side of the AFV. He aimed roughly at the markings on the side of the vehicle, which quickly swerved and ground to a halt. Tensely, Ridgeway waited for the enemy crew to fire or attempt to capture him. Nothing happened. He waited for a moment, and then approached. The crew inside was dead.

Ridgeway, Gavin, Taylor, and many others exhibited the Airborne's famous can-do attitude and the belief that the mission was all-important. The legacy of the Airborne's service and determination has defined the attitude of the men who train today's United States Armed Forces. The difficult they did at once. The impossible took a little longer. These were the men who flew to war and walked home.

COLOR PLATE COMMENTARY

PLATE A: JUMP SCHOOL TRAINING, FT BENNING, AUTUMN 1942

A lieutenant has failed to follow instructions to the 'T' and his instructor has told him to drop and do 25 push-ups. Jump School training included push-ups and five-mile runs – and then jumps from the training tower prior to jumps from an airplane. After the first week, trainees were so inured to the ever-popular push-up that many times they dropped immediately, did their twenty-five and then popped back to attention as the drill sergeant watched. Students ran everywhere. When jumping in a simulated air drop from the tower, the instructor on the ground yelled up to the student to change his D-ring from his right hand to his left one (probably to see if the student had his wits about him) before he landed. If the student failed to respond, not only did he make another jump from the tower, he also had to do a few push-ups. Every trainee made at least two descents from the tower. The drill instructor, whether officer or NCO, was the boss – and officers, NCOs, and enlisted men were equally subject to the same discipline that he meted out to any trainee.

PLATE B: SERGEANT, 506TH PIR, 101ST AIRBORNE, 5 JUNE 1944

Paratroopers had to jump with all their personal kit on them: the sheer quantity of equipment carried often made boarding the plane a difficult procedure. Sometimes items of personal kit were shared between two paratroopers: when one was 'overloaded' with weapons or equipment, he would carry the minimum personal items, and his buddy would carry the rest for him, along with his own.

This sergeant, fully laden with kit for the D-Day drop, has the helmet markings of the 1st Battalion, 506th PIR, and the divisional shoulder patch. Note his face and clothing are heavily camouflaged: he carries the cut-down entrenching tool, and a medical swab attached to his helmet. Over 1,000 transports participated in the D-Day operation. Paratroopers had to contend with the dangers of heavy enemy fire, treacherous landing terrain (town centers and woodlands) and disorientation: many landed far from their designated drop zones.

1 World War 2 manufactured M1910 pattern canteen cover. 2 M1942 aluminum canteen, and M1942 pattern cup with hooks to allow fixing to belt. 3 Map pouch for escape and evasion: this contained a map of Normandy coastline, a compass and a small saw blade. 4 M1936 'musette' field bag. 5 Cigarettes, Zippo lighter; ration packs, soap, laces, shaving brush, razor, comb, toothbrush and toothpaste, bath towel and handkerchief. 6 French currency. 7 1943 identification ('dog') tags and chain. 8 Wrist-worn compass, with leather strap. 9 Spoon. 10 First pattern parachutist's rope coil (c. 33ft/10.05m long). 11 Mk-II A1 fragmentation grenade. 12 Cricket; the 'double-click' sound was used for attracting the attention of fellow airborne troops at night or in poor visibility. 13 M1A1 Thompson sub-machine gun, with 30-round magazine below. 14 A 20-round Thompson magazine pouch. 15 Carton of .45 ammo, and single round. 16 3x30-round and 5x20-round .45 magazine pouches. 17 30-round .45 magazine bag with strap (carries up to 8 magazines). 18 M15 White phosphorous smoke grenade (often employed as an anti-personnel grenade). 19 M18 colored smoke grenade. 20 Survival kit, containing food, fire lighters, and other basic survival items. 21 First-aid pouch, containing a dressing and morphine. 22 Morphine solution and syrette. 23 Field dressing, and tourniquet. 24 M5 black gas mask, and M7 black rubberized canvas carrying bag. 25 M3 trench knife and M6 scabbard: usually this was attached to the lower leg. 26 M1910 entrenching tool and cloth cover. 27 B4 ('Mae West') life preserver. 28 101st Airborne Division shoulder patch.

PLATE C: PATHFINDER TEAM A, 502ND REGT. 101ST AIRBORNE; ST GERMAIN-DE-VARREVILLE, NORMANDY, 0030 HRS 6 JUNE 1944

Pathfinder teams were drawn from their parent regiments, and underwent special group training for navigation awareness and night jumping. They were tasked with marking drop zones for their fellow paratroopers, by lights, fire, or radio 'homing' beacons. First deployed in Italy, at Salerno, in 1943, they played a key role in the Normandy drops.

In this scene, the A Team of 18 pathfinders of 502nd Regt 101st Airborne, led by Capt Frank Lillyman, have landed in the outskirts of the town of St Germain-de-Varreville on D-Day, 6 June 1944. Lillyman's team jumped at 0015 hrs and landed east of Ste Mère Eglise, in Drop Zone A. Their orders were strictly to do no shooting and to take evasive action if discovered. This group of Pathfinders comprised the first troops to land on D-Day in France. Lillyman always jumped with a cigar in his mouth.

The Pathfinders are in a field in the outskirts of the Cotentin peninsula town, and are about to set up the T-lights to indicate the drop zone for the main parachute landings, and the three PPN2 Rebecca-Eureka radio transmitters to guide the planes in. 14 men set up the beacons and the 7 electric Aldis lights in T-formation, whilst the other four men kept lookout for approaching enemy troops. The three beacons that the team carried (radio homing devices) were set up in the bushes near the church. The 7 Aldis lights in T-formation were laid out 200 yds east of the 3 radio beacons, in the middle of the open field, a visual marker to guide the men and planes in. These lights were not turned on until 0040 hrs though: once on, they remained lit for 47 minutes whilst the Pathfinders waited for the drop to materialize – a long wait indeed, but they were not disturbed or discovered by German troops.

PLATE D: A: GLIDER INFANTRY OFFICER OF 325TH GIR, 82ND AIRBORNE. B: GLIDER PILOT, 6 JUNE 1944

The primary aircraft used for carrying airborne troops and equipment were the C-47 Douglas, or 'Gooney Bird' as it was affectionately nicknamed, and the 'Waco' CG-4A Glider. The C-47s were used to transport personnel and cargo and, in a combat role, for towing troop-carrying gliders and dropping paratroopers into enemy territory. The 'Waco' CG-4A was the most widely used US troop/cargo glider of the war. It was constructed of fabric-covered wood and metal and was crewed by a pilot and co-pilot. It could carry 13 troops and their equipment or either a jeep, a quarter-ton truck, or a 75mm howitzer loaded through the upward-hinged nose section. C-46s and C-47s were usually used as the tow aircraft. The gliders themselves were often considered expendable in combat and few efforts were made to retrieve them.

Glider troops and pilots suffered heavy combat losses (as did the pilots and troops of tow planes). They were towed in flimsy, noisy, unarmed aircraft at about 130 mph at the end of a 300 ft. 1-inch nylon rope in air made turbulent by the tow planes. They sometimes crash-landed at night in small fields behind enemy lines, carrying troops and/or cargo including jeeps and artillery. Landing in a glider was a risky procedure. Even if the pilot had the time and altitude to select a good spot to land, conditions on the ground could present significant problems, and the landing terrain was rarely smooth or tree-free: ditches, wire, fences, tree stumps or rocks could flip, twist, or decimate a glider. The landing procedure was little more than a controlled crash: on contact with the ground, the gliders tipped forward and metal skid brakes were applied to bring them to a halt. At D-Day, the Germans planted poles in the fields too, which ripped the wings off many gliders causing significant casualties.

Glider pilots were unique in that they had no parachutes, no motors, and no second chances. Glider training was usually conducted in three phases. The first consisted of approximately 60 hours in light aircraft; the second, approximately 30 hours in small sailplanes; and the last phase, 60 hours in the type glider to be flown in combat, the CG-4A. Most graduates then were given overseas assignments with troop carrier units. Glider pilots received training in infantry combat tactics too, since after landing they were sometimes required to fight as infantry. Despite being attached to airborne regiments, glider troops were mostly kited out with standard infantry clothing and equipment.

1 M1941 field jacket. 2 M1 helmet. 3 Above, .30 cal M1 carbine: below, .30 cal M1A1 carbine with folding metal stock. 4 Infantry boots, and 5 infantry leggings, with 17 eyelets. 6 Tent shelter half, with poles and pegs. 7 M1911 A1 Colt .45 cal pistol, plus M1916 pattern leather (belt) holster. 8 M4-10-6 Lightweight Service Gas Mask, with carrying bag, and waterproofing kit and demister (below). 9 M1928 haversack. 10 82nd Airborne Division shoulder patch. 11 Compass pouch for belt attachment, and 12 compass. 13 USAAF shoulder patch. 14 M1910 pickmattock; head, handle and cover. 15 M1910 hand axe, with cover. 16 M1936 wire-cutters and pouch.

PLATE E: PARATROOPER CLOTHING

Paratrooper clothing developed during the course of the war, in the light of lessons learned in combat and different environments. Many items used retained the status of standard infantry issue, but others were specifically adapted to the needs of the paratrooper in the field.

1 M1942 jump jacket with reinforced pockets and elbows. 2 M1942 jump trousers with reinforced pockets and knee patches. 3 M1943 jacket. 4 M1943 modified trousers with braces and leg ties. 5 Corcoran (left) and Goodrich (right) jump boots, showing details of their heels/soles. 6 M1943 buckle boots, standard issue by late 1944. 7 Enlisted man's belt. 8 Woolen caps: above, A4 winter type mechanic's cap, and below M1941 wool knit cap. 9 Sewing kit, shown both 'closed' and 'open'. 10 Undergarments. 11 Trouser braces. 12 Scarf/identification panel, made of white silk. 13 M1944 pattern goggles, and 14 M1943 pattern goggles. 15 M1936 suspenders for cartridge and pistol belts: these gave extra support when heavy equipment was carried, and extra padding was sometimes inserted under the shoulder straps. 16 Horsehide riding gloves, adapted from the cavalry glove. 17 Gas detector armband: this would change color in the vicinity of gas. 18 M2 ammunition bag, worn over the shoulders. 19 Shirts and sweaters. 20 M1936 cartridge belt. 21 Oil cloth arm identification band, with 48 stars.

PLATE F: 75 MM PACK HOWITZER, 457TH PARACHUTE FIELD ARTILLERY BATTALION, CAMP POLK, LOUISIANA, FEBRUARY 1944

The 75 mm M1A1 pack howitzer was ideally suited as the Airborne division's main artillery piece. The '75' was developed in 1923 to be broken down into mule loads and the M8 carriage with modern rubber tires was adopted in 1940 placing the weapon within weight and bulk limitations for parachute and glider delivery. Development of a means to parachute drop the weapon began in September 1942 and was standardized in

May 1943. This system consisted of nine differently designed containers for weapon components, fire control equipment, accessories, and ammunition with each dropped under an individual 24 ft diameter cargo parachute. Sometimes different colored parachutes (white, red, blue, yellow, green, orange) were used to identify certain components or the containers for a specific howitzer. All paracrates were provided with uniquely designed white web parachute suspension harnesses. One complete howitzer, ammunition load, and its crew could be dropped from a single C-47 transport. The M1 to M5 paracrates and M9 paracassion were fitted with bomb shackles and were dropped from racks beneath the plane. The M6 paracrate and M8 parachest with ammunition were pushed from the door and followed by the seven-man crew. The nine loaded containers totaled 2,571 lb.

Three types of ammunition were available for the 75 mm: M48 high explosive (HE), M64 white phosphorus (WP), and M66 high explosive antitank (HEAT). The latter was effective up to 1,500 yds, but could penetrate only 3 in of armor, less than the bazooka.

Howitzer crews spent much of their training time rigging, assembling, and moving their weapons by hand as depicted by this 457th Parachute Field Artillery Battalion crew training for the Pacific Theater at Camp Polk, Louisiana. The M9 paracassion is prepared for hauling and the two boxes making up the M8 parachest have been separated. Once the weapon was assembled for manhandling into position, the ammunition tubes removed from the parachest were often lashed across the howitzer's trail. While glider field artillery battalions were provided a quarter-ton jeep for each pack howitzer, the parachute battalions were not.

PLATE G: DEMOLITION PLATOON PARATROOPER, 82ND AIRBORNE: OPERATION MARKET GARDEN, 17 SEPTEMBER 1944

Parachute infantrymen received special training on assault demolition materials, and were given more extensive demo training than other infantrymen. Certain platoons were tasked with specific demolition roles. Training in communication techniques and signals equipment was equally important: special Signal Corps fulfilled this key role. Such knowledge areas were paramount: the paratrooper in the field needed to be resourceful, given his potentially isolated status.

This figure wears the M1943 jacket and modified trousers with leg ties, and bears the 82nd Airborne patch on his left shoulder. He is armed with the .30 M1 Garand rifle, and wears two light khaki M1 ammo bandoleers across his chest, together with M3 binoculars in the M17 leather case. He carries a demolition pack in his left hand. He is also equipped with the TL-122C flashlight.

1 M1942 bayonet, long (16") with **2** scabbard; **3** standard 10" version. **4** M8 scabbard, with M3 trench knife inside, usually attached to the lower leg. **5** M2 pocket knife (switchblade), with cord. **6** .30 M1 Garand rifle: **7** M7 grenade launcher, for Garand rifle. **8** M1A2 rifle grenade adapter. **9** Garand carrying strap. **10** 8-round clip for M1 rifle, with ammo pouch. **11** M1 Garand cleaning and maintenance tool. **12** Oil bottle and grease bottle, and **13** pull-through cord, for rifle maintenance. **14** Hawkins ATK Light Anti-Tank Mine Mk II: **15** igniter. **16** BC-611 walkie talkie. **17** M1C helmet, with liner: this replaced the earlier M2 helmet. **18** M1943 entrenching tool and **19** cloth cover. **20** CS-34 leather Signal

Corps pouch, with knife inside: this was carried by demolition and Signal Corps paratroopers in particular. **21** M1910 first aid pouch for web belt, two-studded version, front and rear views. **22** M1943 version of first aid pouch. **23** Field dressing. **24** Pigeon leg capsule, and **25** homing-pigeon carrying harness: the Signal Corps used these to convey messages as late as September 1944. **26** Type 2 demolition pack (rear view), plus demolition equipment: **27** detonator cord; **28** time fuse and pull fuse (with ring); **29** C2 demolition block and **30** TNT blocks.

PLATE H: ASSAULT BOAT, 3D BATTALION, 504TH PARACHUTE INFANTRY REGIMENT; WAAL RIVER, THE NETHERLANDS, 20 SEPTEMBER 1944

The earlier failed attempts to capture the Wall River highway and railroad bridges at Nijmegen led to a desperate attempt at 1400 hrs on 20 September by two companies of the 3d Battalion, 504th PIR. Folding canvas assault boats were provided 20 minutes before H-Hour by the Royal Engineers. The paratroopers, unfamiliar with the 137-lb, 12-ft-long, 4-ft-wide boats, carried them over a dike then across a wide, flat shore to the river while artillery and aircraft pounded the enemy side. Halfway across the 400-yd-wide river a brisk wind blew away the smoke screen, completely exposing the 32 boats. The fast 10-mph current was too much for the boats' five paddles and the nine paratroopers in each, now exposed to heavy machine-gun and mortar fire, frantically used their rifles to paddle across. Half of the boats were destroyed or so shot-up as to be unable to return for more troops. Small groups of survivors fought their way to the north end of the bridges while the 505th PIR, supported by British tanks, overwhelmed defenders on the south end. Close to 300 Germans were killed at the bridges, but the 504th lost 200 of its own, resulting in the award of the Presidential Unit Citation.

PLATE I: TANK HUNTER/KILLER TEAM, 507TH PIR, WESEL, GERMANY 1945

The 17th Airborne Division's 24 March 1945 airborne assault, Operation Varsity, across the Rhine River placed the division in an exposed position north of Wesel, Germany. The paratroopers faced piecemeal German tank attacks on the first day resulting in the destruction of 13 tanks and two assault guns.

Major Royal Taylor photographed at Frankfurt-am-Main, where he headed a security company of the 508th for Gen Eisenhower at the end of the war. Although Taylor is wearing only a few of his decorations, he does wear his hard-earned jump wings – something no paratrooper would be without. (Author's collection)

With the appearance of the 2.36-in M1 antitank rocket launcher, or bazooka, in 1942 the US infantryman was for the first time provided with a lightweight weapon capable of knocking out most tanks. By 1944, the much improved M9 and M9A1 versions of the bazooka were in wide use (M9A1 had an improved barrel coupling). This version was specifically requested by the Airborne command as the one-piece barrel M1 and M1A1 were difficult to jump with. The M9 had a two-piece barrel allowing it to be broken down for jumping and non-tactical carrying. This feature also allowed for a longer barrel increasing range and accuracy.

Bazookas were not allocated dedicated crews, but units established their own organizational practices to man them. A bazooka required a two-man crew, the gunner and loader allowing them to keep up a 4–5 round-per-minute sustained rate of fire. A practiced crew could deliver as many as 10 rounds in a minute. Tank hunter/killer teams, usually built around a rifle squad, were frequently deployed forward of friendly lines to ambush enemy armor and reconnaissance vehicles. Their tactics were straightforward; lie-in wait until an enemy patrol accompanied by one or two armored vehicles approached, engage them at close range, and immediately withdraw – hit and run. It was found that when German armored vehicles were smoked they often withdrew as this portended a close attack. If the enemy proved resolute the bazooka crew would use the smoke to close in for the kill while the remainder of the team, supported by a BAR or light machine-gun, provided covering fire.

The M7 grenade launcher fitted on an M1 rifle provided a valuable addition to the hunter/killer team. The M9A1 antitank grenade could penetrate 3-4 in of armor at up to 250 yds. Enemy vehicles were blinded by M19A1 white phosphorus (WP) smoke grenades. Besides dense screening smoke, burning WP particles could cause casualties within 15 yds. M22 red smoke grenades, also provided in yellow, violet, and green, were used to mark targets and burned for about one minute after impact.

Besides the M6A1/A2 antitank rockets, the bazooka was provided with other rounds. The M6A1 was a factory produced, improved version of the deficient M6 while the M6A2 was an M6 modified to A1 standards in the theater of operations by ordnance teams. The M6A3 rocket was a completely redesigned round with improved penetration and reliability. The M10 WP rocket, which saw only limited use, was used for the same purpose as the M19A1 WP grenade. Three rockets were carried in the M6 parachutist's rocket-carrying bag. This differed from standard bags with the addition of a V-ring, snap-hook, and leg tie-tapes to securely fasten it to jumpers.

1st Sgt Leonard A. Funk Jr. (Co.C, 508th PIR) is awarded the congressional Medal of Honor, which is being pinned on him by Maj Gen James ('Slim Jim') Gavin, commander of the 82nd Airborne. Funk had already been awarded a Silver Star and a DSC. (Author's collection)

PLATE J: JUMP EQUIPMENT AND TEAM WEAPONS

Individual and crew-served weapons training was a continuous process going beyond simply initial qualification firing. A paratrooper was cross-trained to operate every weapon in his company along with some of the enemy's basic weapons. Besides individual proficiency with weapons, the employment of multiple types of weapons in different tactical situations and types of terrain, day and night, was emphasized. This was conducted in unit live-fire training exercises from squad through regimental-levels to familiarize soldiers and leaders on how to most effectively employ their weapons in different situations and to take advantage of their capabilities and understand their limitations.

1 T5 parachute, underside view; **1a** harness; **1b** belly band, **1c** static line (15 ft long). **2** Front view (smaller scale) of T5 chute, with extended belly band. **3** Detail of T5 1944 modified harness, showing the 'quick release' buckle. **4** Reserve chute underside view and **5** front view. **6** M1A1 carbine holster case, with weapon inside. **7** First Pattern Griswold padded weapons case. **8a** Second Pattern bag with M1 Garand dismantled on top. **8b** Second Pattern bag with lengthened section at base, note the leg ties. **9** 1944 leg bag. **10** Parachute log record book, kept with the chute. **11** A5 delivery container, and **12** marker light (also shown attached to right end of bag, in actual scale). **13a** AL-140 identification panel, and **13b** CS-150 carrying case. Below are shown (in smaller scale) some of the common signals created; **14** 'we are attacking'; **15** 'need ammo'; and **16** 'the enemy is attacking'. **17** M3 utility hand cart, with canvas cover. **18** Modified M6 bazooka bag, and **19** M9 bazooka: **20** 2.36 in HE round. **21** .30 cal. BAR M1918 A2. **22** .30 Browning M1919A4 light machine-gun, with cleaning kit below. **23** Ammo can for Browning LMG. **24** M2 60mm mortar, with **25** M4 optics inside leather case. **26** HE round for mortar.

INDEX

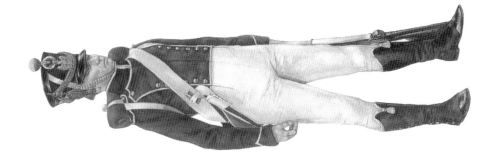 

OSPREY
PUBLISHING

FIND OUT MORE ABOUT OSPREY

❏ Please send me the latest listing of Osprey's publications

❏ I would like to subscribe to Osprey's e-mail newsletter

Title / rank

Name

Address

City / county

Postcode / zip   state / country

e-mail

WAR

I am interested in:

❏ Ancient world
❏ Medieval world
❏ 16th century
❏ 17th century
❏ 18th century
❏ Napoleonic
❏ 19th century

❏ American Civil War
❏ World War 1
❏ World War 2
❏ Modern warfare
❏ Military aviation
❏ Naval warfare

Please send to:

USA & Canada:
Osprey Direct USA, c/o MBI Publishing, P.O. Box 1,
729 Prospect Avenue, Osceola, WI 54020

UK, Europe and rest of world:
Osprey Direct UK, P.O. Box 140, Wellingborough,
Northants, NN8 2FA, United Kingdom

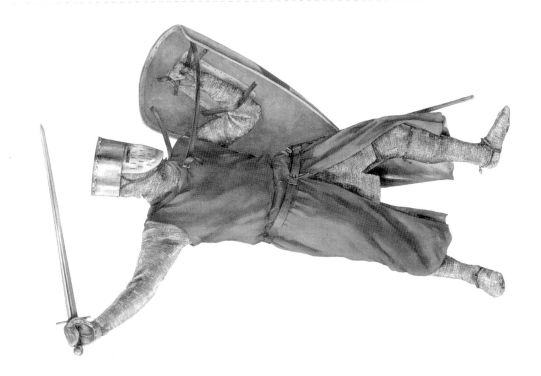

OSPREY
PUBLISHING

www.ospreypublishing.com

call our telephone hotline
for a free information pack

USA & Canada: 1-800-826-6600
UK, Europe and rest of world call:
+44 (0) 1933 443 863

Young Guardsman
Figure taken from *Warrior 22:
Imperial Guardsman 1799–1815*
Published by Osprey
Illustrated by Richard Hook

Knight, c.1190
Figure taken from *Warrior 1: Norman Knight 950 – 1204 AD*
Published by Osprey
Illustrated by Christa Hook

POSTCARD